D1595565

THE UNITED STATES

EARLY SILVER DOLLARS

1794 to 1803

JULES REIVER

Published by

krause publications

700 E. State Street - Iola, WI 54900-0001

Telephone: 715-445-2214

Please call or write for our free catalog. Our toll-free number to place an order or obtain a free catalog is 800-258-0929 or please use our regular business telephone 715-445-2214 for editorial comment and further information.

ISBN: 0-87341-602-3
Printed in the United States of America

Table of Contents

Acknowledgments

I should like to thank the following numismatists for their help in producing this book:

Mark Borckardt
Kenneth Bressett
John Darmanin
John Haugh
Jim Matthews
James McConnell
Eric Newman
W. David Perkins
David Queller
Iona Reiver
Bob Stark
Bowers & Merena Galleries
Krause Publications

...and for two who have passed on

Walter Breen
Jack Collins

Preface

The United States Silver Dollars from 1794 to 1803

The first silver dollars of the United States have been a collectors' item for at least a hundred and fifty years. The *Annual Report of the Director of the Mint* gives the total dollars struck from 1793 through 1805 as 1,439,517. As I remember it, the last figure, 321 dollars struck in 1805, was a case of that quantity of silver brought to the mint to be converted to silver dollars, but, since no 1805 dies were available, the silver was returned unstruck. This would reduce the total to 1,439,296, which is probably the correct figure.

The earliest information I have seen is the *Catalogue of John W. Haseltine Type Table—U.S. Dollars, Half Dollars & Quarter Dollars*[1], The book included: United States and Foreign Gold; Silver and Bronze Medals; Jacksonian Tokens; Ancient Coins; Pattern Pieces; Fractional Currency; Confederate Bonds; War Envelopes; Autographs; Proof Sets; United States Cents and Half Cents; Colonials, etc. to be sold at auction by Messrs. Bangs & Co., at their salesrooms, nos. 739 and 741 Broadway, New York, on Monday, Tuesday, and Wednesday afternoons, November 28, 29, & 30, 1881.

Excellent descriptions were given for the Dollars, Half Dollars, and Quarters, with the rest of the items being sold merely listed. The Bust Dollars were the first described in the book, covering pages 3 through 16, lots 78-187, or 110 coins. This was probably every known variety, when you consider that only 116 varieties are known today. Each coin, in addition to having a complete description, had a variety number in addition to the lot number. Haseltine deserves much credit for a pioneering book.

Bolender issued his book in 1950, and I managed to get an autographed copy. It was based on Haseltine's work, and was very nicely done. It has gone through five editions.

The next book is a tremendous two volume set by Q. David Bowers in 1993, which covers all of the dollars struck by the United States from 1794 through 1996. It has the most complete information available. Bowers used a new numbering system, which follows the emission sequence more closely. I chose to use Haseltine—Bolender numbers for the coins, but did, however, prepare mating charts, which use Bowers numbers and letters to identify the dies used for each variety. I find these to be very helpful, and hope that others will find this also.

Although Bolender discussed the 1804 dollar, he opined that those struck with that date were actually made many years later.

In revisions of the book, I did add some information about, and pictures of, the 1804 dollar. However, since records show that they were not struck until 1834, it seems reasonable that they should be excluded from this series.

Anyone desiring to learn more about them should read *The Fantastic 1804 Dollar* by Eric P. Newman and Kenneth E. Bressett, issued in 1962 by Whitman Publishing Co. in Racine, Wisconsin.

In 1986, at The American Numismatic Society, Newman and Bressett presented a 25th Anniversary follow-up, including additional information. This is probably still available from the ANS.

[1] *Printed in 1881 by Bavis and Pennypacker, Steam Power Printers, No. 23 S. Tenth St., Philadelphia.*

Introduction

by W. David Perkins

Milferd H. Bolender wrote, in the original 1950 introduction to his book *The United States Early Silver Dollars from 1794 to 1803,* "The early silver dollars of the United States have long enjoyed ever increasing popularity among both new and advanced collectors in this country." Prior to the publication of this landmark book, most collectors were content collecting early dollars by date and major type of obverse and reverse. Bolender's book had the effect of popularizing collecting the dollars by "Bolender" variety in the 1950s and beyond.

The first attempt to categorize the early dollars by die variety was published by John W. Haseltine in November, 1881 and is known as the *Haseltine Type Table*. Haseltine included his *Type Table* as part of the auction sale catalog in which he sold his own collection of early silver dollars. Numismatists and researchers today question if Haseltine's *Type Table* was not really, all or in part, the work of J. Colvin Randall. A portion of Randall's collection of early silver dollars (and other coins) were offered in W. Elliot Woodward's 77th Sale, June 29-July 1, 1885.
Woodward states in this catalog that in a private letter to him, Mr. Randall wrote "The idea of a correct work on types and varieties of United States silver dollars, halves and quarters, originated with me. H. (referring to Haseltine) and myself were to publish the work together, but without any consultation whatever with me, he issued for his own benefit what he styles the *Type Table Catalogue*." Regardless of who should be credited with this work, there were no plates included in the *Type Table* and it was very difficult to attribute varieties using only the descriptions provided in this reference. John J. Ford stated this well in his October, 1950, review of Bolender's book which appeared in *The Numismatist*. Ford wrote "Haseltine's list, while quite complete, and generally systematic, was no doubt composed with all of the coins available for careful comparison. While comparatively satisfactory for a patient man with a large number of coins to catalog, Haseltine often proved extremely difficult for one man with but two or three specimens to attribute."

Bolender's book was a big improvement over the *Haseltine Type Table*. Bolender made corrections, enhanced descriptions, and added new varieties and die states. Bolender retained the Haseltine numbering system but called the coins Bolender numbers (H-1 became B-1, etc.). Most importantly, he added plates of all obverse and reverse dies known to him using specimens from his own collection. Lastly, he added rarity ratings for the die varieties.

Bolender sold his private collection of early dollars in his 183rd Auction Sale on Saturday, February 23, 1952. Offered in this sale were 183 varieties of early dollars before 1804! Bolender stated in his introduction that "Interested bidders can see the plates in the book of the exact coins here listed, and together with this catalogue and a price list after the sale, this will be a complete and accurate guide to the early dollars...Prospective bidders should order a book now, and enjoy studying same before placing bids. The plates should be very helpful, to see the high quality of the coins." This was the most complete variety collection of early dollars ever formed and offered for sale. It is notable for the large number of varieties, subvarieties (different die states) as well as pedigrees. Many of these dollars came from famous collections including Stickney, Parmelee, Earle, Gable, Mougey, Newcomer, Col. Green, World's Greatest Collection (Boyd) and Jenks. Bolender believed a few specimens were from the Haseltine collection, however they were identified as "probably from the Haseltine collection" due to their rarity and condition. Very few early dollars have turned up definitively pedigreed to Haseltine's collection. Where are they today?

Around the time Bolender was selling his collection, others were starting or adding to their early dollar collections. Great die variety collections were being formed by noted specialists such as Frank Sterling, Emanuel Taylor, K.P. Austin, Farish Baldenhofer, Andre DeCoppet and W. Earl Spies. In the 1950s and 1960s, Alfred J. Ostheimer formed probably the finest and most extensive early dollar variety collection. It was dispersed in various auction sales between 1968 and 1975. Two other extensive variety collections were sold in the last decade, both by Superior Rare Coin Galleries: the Woody Blevins Sale in June, 1988 and the Roland Willach collection in May, 1990. The most complete variety collection existing today is probably that of Jules Reiver. Much of this extensive collection is illustrated in this book. This collection contains all the varieties represented in Bolender's collection, a few that were missing, and a number of varieties discovered after the publication of Bolender's book in 1950 and the selling of Bolender's collection in 1952.

Bolender's book has served collectors and dealers well for almost fifty years. This revision is much needed and should be appreciated by all who use it. The plates are significantly improved over the first five editions with new photos, taken by Jules Reiver and published using modern technology. Plates now accompany the variety descriptions in the text. The variety descriptions have been updated with new "keys" to identify the variety. Varieties will be much easier to attribute using the "rapid finder" developed and refined by Jules Reiver over the last thirty years, published for the first time here. We hope you find the book useful and enjoyable!

W. David Perkins, NLG
Littleton, Colorado
March, 1998

Overview of Early Dollars Varieties

by John J. Haugh

One of the more fascinating aspects of early dollar study and collecting is the extraordinary variety of designs, die varieties, and die states. They present a special challenge and have some aspects not found in other US "types." Among the more notable:

Silver Plug

Some (most believe thirty to fifty, a few surmise eighty or more) of the Flowing Hair dollars minted in 1795 have a silver "plug" in the center, visible on both sides. Thus far, they have been found in five varieties (B-1, 3, 4, 7 and 9). Roughly 8mm in diameter, and always found at or close to the center of the coin, this curious anomaly was not mentioned in any of the books or articles on Flowing Hair dollars, for nearly 200 years. Both John W. Haseltine and M. H. Bolender—in their seminal studies—missed it.

Although many noted numismatists are given (or try to take credit) for having "discovered" the silver plugged variety, anecdotal stories convincingly demonstrate that "coin doctors" were the first to encounter the plug decades ago when—in the process of attempting to improve their appearance—a "circle" would "pop" out of some 1795s after heating. One coin doctor—long since retired—confided to me he had experienced that phenomenon three times. He gently tapped the popout back into the coin. For obvious reasons, this group did not report their findings to the coin media.

Bowers described the curiosity in 1981, but was unsure what it was. By the early 1990s, several numismatists began to delve into the enigmatic "small circle" found in some 1795 Flowing Hair dollars, including Bowers, Roger Burdette, Kenneth Bressett and Tom DeLorey. Initially, it was surmised some indentation or defect in planchets had been corrected, then covered with silver. As more examples surfaced, more attention was focused on the strange anomaly.

Bressett presented a paper on the "curious circular ring or seam" at the October 1993 American Numismatic Society (ANS) Coinage of the America's Conference (COAC) focusing on Americaís Silver Coinage. After analysis of numerous examples, all the same size and in the same location, he found they had all been added before striking, as the die impressions were always struck over them. Bressett and Burdette speculated that the strange metal had been added to increase the silver content (fineness).

It was known, from earlier research, that the Mint director (David Rittenhouse) had ignored the silver fineness mandated by Congress (.89243) and secretly employed a .900 benchmark, adding an extra 3.5 grains of silver to each silver dollar coin. Could Rittenhouse have added a tad of metal to planchets to come into compliance with the mandated standard? This was originally thought to be the answer.

As Bressett studied the circular ring further, he soon concluded it was far more probable that extra metal was added to bring lightweight planchets up to standard. He reasoned the extra metal brought those "short" up to the norm, at least as an experiment in 1795, just as overweight planchets were corrected by removing metal with a fine file, leaving adjustment marks. The plug is not found in 1794, the Draped Busts of 1795, or any subsequent year.

The plug area was subjected to spectrographic x-ray analysis, which demonstrated the fineness of the added metal roughly equaled the rest of the planchet in nearly all cases (or was within understandable tolerances of). In reality, the term "plug" is somewhat misleading. Bressett explains his conclusion as to how the metal was added in the paper described above, as follows:

During mid-1795, an experiment was tried in the mint to salvage lightweight planchets by inserting a dowel, or plug, in the center of the piece and then striking it with normal dies. There would be no need to drill a hole, or remove any metal. A simple piercing with a sharp instrument would leave an opening where a pin or dowel could be inserted. The effect after striking would be to round over the exposed tips on each side of the coin, much like the ends of rivets used in building construction...

Copper pattern cents of 1792 also have a "silver center" from a dowel inserted prior to striking (to raise the coin value to face); no other regular issue of the US Mint was known to have a silver "plug." However, in 1997, a 1795 Flowing Hair half dollar was discovered to have a similar plug. A second was soon found. Other 1795 halves with this feature will probably surface; the hunt for them is on in earnest.

Chris Pilliod, a professional metallurgist and numismatic historian, subjected the "discovery" 1795 half dollar with silver plug to advanced electron analysis. After five readings on each side, he found the silver fineness and trace metals to be virtually the same for the plug and the remainder of the coin. He concluded the "plugging was undoubtedly done solely as a weight adjustment on light planchets" prior to striking.

Why did the 1795 Flowing Hair dollar (and half) with silver plug go "undiscovered" for some 200 years? One can only surmise. In early America, coins were often holed for jewelry, pocket pieces and coat buttons. Many were plugged later, often expertly. Some who noticed the circle may have assumed this had occurred. Moreover, the outline of the plug is nearly (or completely) invisible on darkly-toned specimens. Even professional numismatists, who noticed the curious circle, dismissed it as "toning." As late as October 1992, when the noted Starr collection was auctioned by Stack's, the catalogue described a silver plugged 1795 dollar as having "a splash of toning, mostly in the central portions of each side." The overwhelming consensus today is that the "plugs" were inserted prior to striking to correct light planchets, in an experiment which occurred only in 1795. The *Red Book* began listing the "silver center plug" as a separate variety in 1994. It commands a premium over common varieties of 1795 Flowing Hair Dollars in the same condition.

Adjustment Marks

Except for 1795, when many Flowing Hair dollars received the "silver plug" treatment, underweight planchets were added to the bullion inventory, remelted, and put through the process again (forming ingots, rolling them into strips, and punching out planchets). Overweight planchets were dealt with in a different manner, and are much more common. Overweight planchets were lightened, prior to striking, by creating thin grooves into the metal with a fine file to remove metal.

Thousands of early dollars show this hand filing, which appear as "scratches" or thin grooves. Most are parallel. Some "criss-cross." Some are quite prominent, even unsightly. Some are almost invisible, nearly obliterated in the striking process. Over the years, specialists have come to refer to these filing grooves as "adjustment marks." They appear on many dates and varieties. Most of the surviving 1794 issue bear adjustment marks on the obverse.

Most collectors, especially those seeking attractive "type" pieces, consider adjustment marks a detriment. A few specialists actively seek early dollars with dramatic adjustment marks as examples of the early Mint process. In 1996, Bowers and Merena reported, in their "Rare Coin Review" for collectors, that Ray Merena had found a 1795 Flowing Hair (BB-18/B-7) with both a silver plug and adjustment marks. Bressett opined that the coin may have been made too light by filing, then brought back to standard by plugging. This writer wonders if it could have been the reverse? It was the only known 1795 with both a silver plug and adjustment marks until 1998, when a second one was found. Other examples may exist.

Edge Lettering

The purpose of the Flowing Hair and Draped Bust dollar was to create a coin containing one dollar's worth of silver. Silver (and gold) were the medium of exchange. For centuries, people would file, clip or "shave" small amounts of silver or gold off the edges of coins, gradually accumulating significant amounts of bullion, representing real buying power and value. This "debasement" of the coinage often went undetected. Repeated edge shaving eventually would become apparent, resulting in refusals to accept the coins for goods, defeating their very purpose.

To prevent the filing of edges, and confirm the value of the coins, all early dollars have an inscription incused into the edge, covering the 360 degrees of the perimeter, with ornamental designs between the words. This incused inscription has become known as "edge lettering." The words themselves read: HUNDRED CENTS ONE DOLLAR OR UNIT.

The edge lettering was impressed into the edges by a machine designed to pull the planchet between two steel bars, parallel to each other, each with one half of the inscription and symbols. This edge lettering process rather effectively reduced the penchant to "shave" valuable silver off edges. Such tampering was immediately obvious. As the incusion took place, essentially "pinching" or squeezing the coin, the pressure also raised the outside edge, creating an elevated rim.

Edge lettering is rarely examined closely, even by specialists. Although the edge lettering is impossible to see in certification service "holders", it is frequently found with unusual characteristics. Examples include double (and even triple) punched edges, and "over-runs" (with extra lettering). Examples with reverse lettering (with one or both halves of the inscription pointed the wrong way) exist, probably created when coins were ejected, then returned "backwards" in the machine.

Bifurcation

Bolender, in his important treatise on early dollars, utilized the term "bifurcation" often when describing the characteristics of varieties. He used the term to describe letters and numerals which appear to be "split" or "forked" at the base. He created sub-varieties (such as the 1799 B10b) where he noted bifurcated lettering, whereas the main number (his "non-bifurcated" state) had none. His writing suggests he believed bifurcation was the result of worn dies (a different "die state") or repunching.

Most early dollar collectors and specialists now ignore the term bifurcation as a diagnostic of varieties, though the term is used to describe the "splitting' or "forring" of letters and numerals. In reality, the striking process (which Bolender did not fully understand) created the differentiation in the base of letters and numerals. Reiver and many other specialists believe it is caused by "strong strikes", asserting that if strongly struck, the base of these expand outward, creating "forks", "splits" or "elongations" at the base of letters and numerals (as well as stars) where the planchet tended to flow toward the collar. Bowers and many other specialists assert these same characteristics result from "weak" strikes, when opposing dies do not put sufficient pressure on the planchet. This writer's observations suggest that when the forking or splitting appear, the strike details are invariably stronger. The issue (whether caused by a "strong" or "weak" strike) is worthy of further analysis.

Bolender was unaware of the striking processing intricacies, the detailed research of which was largely done after his work was completed. Specialists now agree that bifurcation is not indicative or diagnostic of die varieties or die states. Indeed, many early dollars of the same die variety and die state can be found with no, little, or heavy bifurcation.

Suction Marks/Die Clashes

Another term used liberally by Bolender, which has confused two generations of early dollar collectors, is "suction marks." As one of the diagnostics of 1799 B-16a, he explains "suction marks . . show between stars on left to stars on right of obverse." What he describes as "suction marks" has been discarded by specialists, who now recognize that they are clash marks. When they noticed the problem, the Mint staff would remove the clash marks by filing, lapping or polishing the dies, which frequently weakened the devices.

Die clashes or die clash marks (or impressions) are found on numerous early dollar varieties. When opposing dies would meet (clash) with no planchet between them, the occurrence would often leave an impression on the opposing die (and sometimes both). If strong enough, this would leave impressions (from faint to strong) on planchets subsequently processed through the altered die.

Interesting Varieties of Early Dollar

Many collectors, especially those putting together "type" sets, purchase two or three early dollars, usually a Flowing Hair and Draped Bust (often including one or two separate examples of the Draped Bust, with the Heraldic Eagle and "Small Eagle" reverse.) Others strive to assemble examples of the *Red Book* varieties (thirty-three, excluding the 1794 proof restrikes and the 1804). Some collect by date. Some focus on gathering an example of every variety of a particular date. A smaller number set out to assemble examples of all the known die varieties (presently 120, including the "Novodel" proofs of 1801-03), a virtually impossible achievement given that sixteen to twenty varieties are presently believed to have a rarity factor of seven (four to twelve examples known) or eight (one to three examples known). Those who have exhausted that effort, or can't afford the extremely rare varieties, sometimes then pursue different die states of the same varieties, which number in the hundreds. The early dollar series presents collectors with a fascinating array of distinct varieties. A brief summary of the more popular and interesting ones follows:

OVERDATES: Overdates exist for two years, the 1799 over 8 (also found with thirteen and fifteen star reverses) and the 1802 over 1 (also found with "narrow" or "thin" and "wide" or "thick" dates). There are three varieties of the 1799 over 8 (B-1, 2 and 3) and five varieties of the 1802 over 1 (the B-1, 2, 3, 4 and 9). Most 1802 over 1 examples are quite dramatic, plain to the naked eye. The 1799 over 8 usually needs magnification to discern. Both overdates are in the "Red Book." Common variety examples are relatively easy to obtain.

AMERICAI: Two varieties of the 1800 issue, made with the same reverse (B-11 and B-19) have what is popularly known as the "AMERICAI" reverse. On the reverse, spaced evenly after AMERICA is a long, slender line, appearing to be an I without serifs. It is readily apparent to the naked eye, and has been extremely popular with collectors for generations. Bowers opines it was caused by a stray metal piece or punch. Some believe it is damage akin to the "spike chin" on the 1804 half cents. Others assert it is a die chip. It commands a premium over the generic 1800. Bolender gave the B-11 an R-7 rating, exclaiming "Excessively rare variety. It took me thirty-five years to find a specimen!" Over the past four decades, more examples of the B-11 have surfaced, and it now is considered an R-5. The B-19 is relatively plentiful, with a present R-2 rating, the same rating as set forth in Bolender's first edition.

"15 STARS" REVERSE: Two varieties with this reverse are found in the 1799 issue, one for the 1799 over 8 overdate (B-3) and one with the "irregular" 1799 date (B-4), both made from the same reverse die. In addition to the thirteen stars normally seen on reverses, these varieties have tips of star rays "peeking out" from the clouds above, one to the extreme left (most dramatic) and one to the extreme right, often invisible except under magnification. It is assumed the engraver erred by punching fifteen stars—instead of the thirteen required by the design—then attempted (almost successfully) to cover up the mistake by enlarging the clouds to cover two stars. The B-3 is presently rated R-3, the B-4 an R-4. Examples of either can be obtained with effort.

THE 1798 SMALL EAGLE AND 1798 HERALDIC EAGLE VARIETIES: As the 1798 issue was minted, an entirely new reverse design was introduced. The "small eagle" (some say "scrawny eagle") was utilized in three distinctively different styles since 1794. It was replaced with a huge ("Heraldic") eagle, with a large shield covering the lower body, the left claw holding a quiver of arrows and the right claw grasping an olive branch, symbolizing a strong defense coupled with a desire for peace. The small eagle was discontinued and the Heraldic eagle basic design continued, through the end of the series. This transitional year (1798) produced in 33 die varieties, only two with the small eagle reverse (B-1 and B-2). Bolender gave them R-4 and R-5 ratings, respectively. Each is now considered R-3. The B-1 has a thirteen star obverse, the B-2 a fifteen star obverse. Both are more elusive (especially in XF or better) than the present ratings would suggest, because there has been considerable demand by all collectors for specimens of this transitional type. The B-2 is especially difficult to find in higher grades, above VF.

"POCKET" AT THROAT AND "COLLAR" AT NECKLINE: One variety of the 1800 (B-17) (in its intermediate and later die states) has what is popularly described as a "collar" on the neck of Liberty (on the obverse) appearing toward the top of the slope below the neck. It is usually visible to the naked eye and was created by a die clash from the eagle's wing. Examples are plentiful, with an R-1 rating. At least two B-17s exist without the "collar" at the neck. One variety of the 1802 over 1 overdate (B-1) has both a "pocket" at the throat (a "chip" extending out where the jaw and throat meet) and a "collar" on the neckline at the base of the portrait. Each is usually quite visible. B-1s in higher grades (above VF) also have a "dot" in front of the lower lip. This variety is elusive, with a present rating of R-4.

THE 1796 SMALL AND LARGE DATE, SMALL AND LARGE LETTERS: As the 1796 issue was minted, two different sizes of punch were used for the date and the reverse perimeter lettering. As a result, there are three major varieties listed in the *Red Book* (and eight, counting sub-varieties, in Bolender). The three major types of 1796 are: small date with small reverse letters (B-1 and 2), small date with larger letters (B-4 and B-6), and the large date with small letters (B-5). Bolender's B-3, described by him as "small wide date" and small letters, is now believed not to exist. The B-1, 2 and 5 have a present R-4 rating. The B-4 is now considered an R-3, somewhat more plentiful. The B-6 is considered an R-8, essentially impossible to obtain (one to three known). The B-1 and B-2, though both small date with small letters, differ slightly as the B-2 has a wider date.

THE "POINTED" AND "KNOB" 9 OF 1798: The 1798 Draped Bust Heraldic eagle issue has six varieties with a "knob" 9 (a small, round "lump" at the tip) and 27 with a "pointed" end. The knob 9 is considered a separate variety. Examples of each are relatively common, with some varieties of each type now rated R-1 to R-3.

THE SMALL (THIN) AND LARGE (THICK) 3 OF 1803: Two different punches were used to produce the 3 of the 1803 issue, resulting in five die varieties where the top edge of the 3 is "thin", and two (counting the proof restrike) where the top edge is "thick." The difference is slight, but they are popular and listed separately in the *Red Book.* One Bolender variety of the "thin" top (B-2) is now believed not to exist. More common varieties of each are relatively available (R-2 and R-3).

THE 1799 8 X 5 OBVERSE STARS: A curious anomaly, one variety of the 1799 issue (B-23) has an obverse of eight stars left, five right. All others are 7x6. Specialists differ as to how this occurred. Was it a "blundered" die, or an engraver accidentally following the 8x5 pattern of the 1799 gold $10? It is elusive, with a present R-4 rating. The 8x5 obverse star of 1799 is highly sought after by *Red*

Book variety collectors and die variety specialists.

THE 1799 HORIZONTAL DIE CRACK: The early dollar series is replete with varieties and die states, diagnosed by die breaks and/or cracks. Among the most dramatic die crack is the 1799 B-22, with a "monster" die crack completely across the reverse, slightly above the center. An R-5 presently (a small group of B-22s were offered in a Bowers' "Aspen" sale in the late 1980s), it is more elusive than the rating would suggest, because it is highly popular. The 1796 B-6 also has a dramatic reverse die crack, but has a present R-8 rating and is essentially impossible to acquire. The 1798 B-5 (an R-6) also has a prominent reverse die crack, as do occasional examples of other varieties.

THE 1799 BLUNDERED STAR/REVERSE OF 98: This one variety (B-15) is the only 1799 with a "line star pattern" reverse (all stars are aligned in parallel lines) common to the 1798. The reverse is the same used for the 1798 B-24 and 25, with a more dramatic die crack from the bottom end of the olive branch stem to the border. It is now considered an R-3, but somewhat more elusive than the rating would suggest.

1795 FLOWING HAIR *RED BOOK* VARIETIES: In part because of separate listings in the *Red Book,* many collectors actively seek specimens of the "two" and "three" leaf 1795 Flowing Hair types. These are found on the reverse inside the branches, to the left and right of the small eagle. Of the nineteen 1795 Flowing Hair varieties currently known in Bolender, thirteen have two leaves and six have three. The two leaf varieties command a modest premium. Examples abound, as many varieties of each have present ratings of R-1 to R-3. The 1795 "silver center plug", also a separate *Red Book* variety, is difficult to obtain in any grade.

THE 1800 "DOTTED DATE": One variety (B-14) of the 1800s has become popularly known as the "dotted date" and is sought after, in part because it has a separate listing in the *Red Book.* Die pits (raised on the struck coin), looking like dots (but are caused by "rust" spots) appear inside, above, and often just below the first 0 in 1800. They are quite visible, except on heavily worn specimens. They are also found sprinkled around the obverse. Specimens are available, with a present rating of R-3.

THE STAR UNDER BUST ("HIDDEN STAR") of 1795: One variety of the 1795 Flowing Hair, the B-4, has an obverse where the 15th star appears completely under the bust. Some call it the "hidden star" obverse, because it is placed (not hidden) where Liberty's eye could not see it. This is a popular variety with a current R-3 rating, but a bit more elusive because of high demand. Although not listed separately in the *Red Book,* it is tracked separately in *Coin World*'s "Trends" section.

THE "HEAD OF 1794" VARIETIES OF 1795: Because eight varieties of the 1795 Flowing Hair have obverses where Liberty's head includes two low, thick curls (akin, but not identical to the 1794), they are called the "Head of 1794." They are numbers B-3, 4, 7, 9, 11, 18, 20, and 22 (only one of which is known to exist). The B-4 and B-7 are most commonly available, with present R-3 ratings.

There are literally dozens of additional varieties, sub-varieties, and die states worthy of special mention. The above are simply some of the most popular, intriguing, and interesting. The "hunt" is still ongoing. Implausible as it may seem, two "new" die varieties of the 1795 Flowing Hair (the B-21 and 22) were reported in the numismatic media in 1997, 202 years after minting!

Notes

A few changes have been made from previous books. I have used all of these for many years, and hope that the collectors will like them. Bowers' numbers are used to identify obverses, and Bowers' letters are used to identify reverses. Although the variety designations are the ones used by Bolender and Haseltine, I feel that this is a step in the right direction.

On the obverse, star numbers start at the top left side and proceed clockwise around the coin. On the reverse, star numbers start at the top left side—across the top row, then the left side of the second row—across the second row, then the left side of the bottom row.

Instead of saying, "the first A in America", etc., the letters can be identified by numbers, and this would be A2. The numbers start at the lower left, and are: U1-N1-I1-T1-E1-D1-S1-T2-A1-T3-E2-S2-O1-F1-A2-M1-E3-R1-I2-C1-A3.

When I talk about die states, I use small letters, the earliest state, usually perfect being state "a", then, using all lower case letters in alphabetical order. As additional die states are discovered, the letters will change. The only way I can see to make these changes is to put the date after the designation—ie. 1798 B18e—5/15/96. When this happens, all of the original designations following the change will have to be changed also.

For the Heraldic Eagle reverses, I use numbers. See Appendix A. They save quite a bit of writing. Each number replaces several words. I will grant that words can better give the exact location, but I find that the numbers are much easier to use, and are excellent for narrowing down the number of coins to be checked. I developed this system for the late date large cents, and had to issue several editions of the list. I advise users not to expect the numbers to perfectly give the location, and in many cases it could be either of two numbers. The system still cuts the number of coins to be checked tremendously. On the large cent numbers, a friend tried out the system on a computer program, and it works very well.

The die states listed are ones that I own or have inspected. I know that there are many others. I would like to hear about them. The die state list should be updated. My phone and fax is 302-475-5636. The address is:

Jules Reiver
1802 Forrest Rd.
Wilmington, DE 19810

Chapter One:

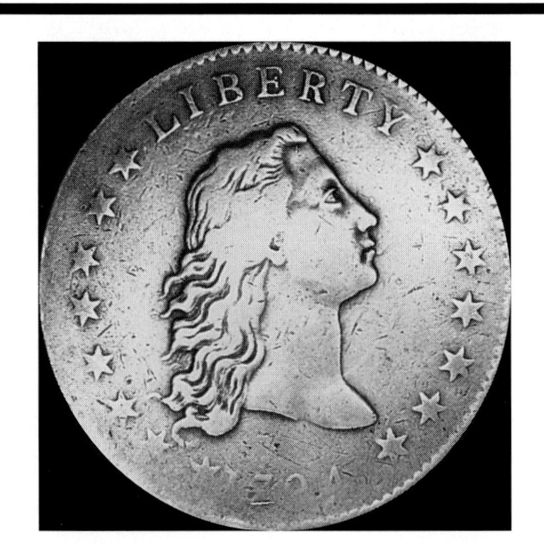

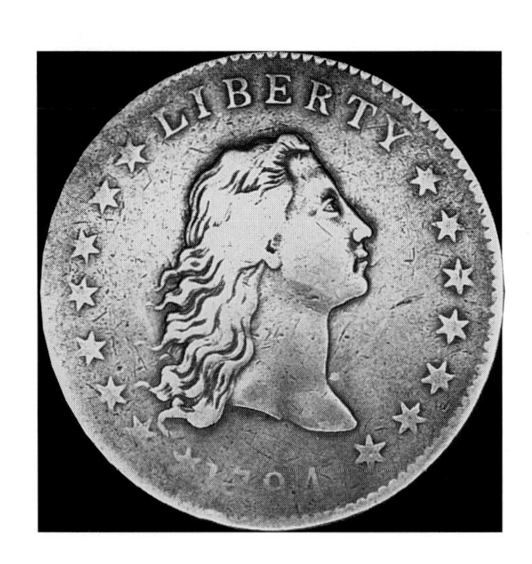

Flowing Hair Type 1794

B1

According to the Mint records, only 1758 dollars were struck in 1794. All the ones that we know of are made from the same die pair. There is at least one piece struck in copper without stars and one in copper with stars. Bolender reports that he had seen one with stars, silver plated.

Most of the examples seen have weak dates, particularly the lower parts, and without the milling on the lower left. The corresponding portion of the reverse, especially the word STATES, is usually weak.

A few years ago, the word passed around that, of the 1758 struck, only 25 to 50 coins were still in existence. Jack Collins was in the process of writing a book about them, listing all of the 1794 dollars known to him. I sent him a picture of the coin bought in 1967 from an ad in *The Numismatist*. When Jack and I ran into each other at an EAC meeting at a Long Beach show, he showed me the page for his book containing my coin. He had listed it as Lot 1028 in the 1982 Stack's Robison sale.

I told Jack that he was wrong, that my coin had been in the safe deposit box since 1967, and was not the Robison coin. Back at home I checked my coin with the excellent picture in Stack's catalog of the Robison Sale, and Jack was correct, the two coins looked exactly alike, with every mark on one also on the other one. I took my coin to Stack's (who were not the ones who sold it to me), who called the buyer of the Robison coin, but he did not know where that piece was. Stack's sent my coin to ANACS, who returned it with papers certifying it as genuine.

My friend Woody Blevins, of Kingsport, Tennessee, introduced me to the executor of his estate, and told him to call me when he passed away, if I was still around, to appraise his coins. Woody died, the executor called me, and I did the appraisal. On seeing the 1794 dollar, I immediately recognized it as the Robison coin. I borrowed it from the executor, and took it home for checking. The two coins were exactly alike. One of them had to be a copy of the other one.

I purchased the coin in the sale of Woody's collection, and sent it in to ANACS, where it too was certified as genuine. At the next ANA Convention, Eric Newman, Walter Breen and I checked the two coins, agreed that one had to be a copy of the other, and that my 1967 coin was the copy of the Blevins coin. I have them as a pair, with instructions that they be sold that way if they are ever sold.

Note: I recently heard a story about the sale of a 1799/8 large cent which was declared a copy and whose pedigree included the same dealer as my 1794 copy. Possibly further investigation could reveal more curious happenings.

OBVERSE First star is close to 1 in date. Second star is near curl, but does not touch it.

REVERSE Twenty-one leaves on each branch. Wreath has ten berries on left branch, nine on right. A leaf touches T3, eagle's wing touches R1.

Rarity 4

Chapter Two:

Rapid Finder for 1795

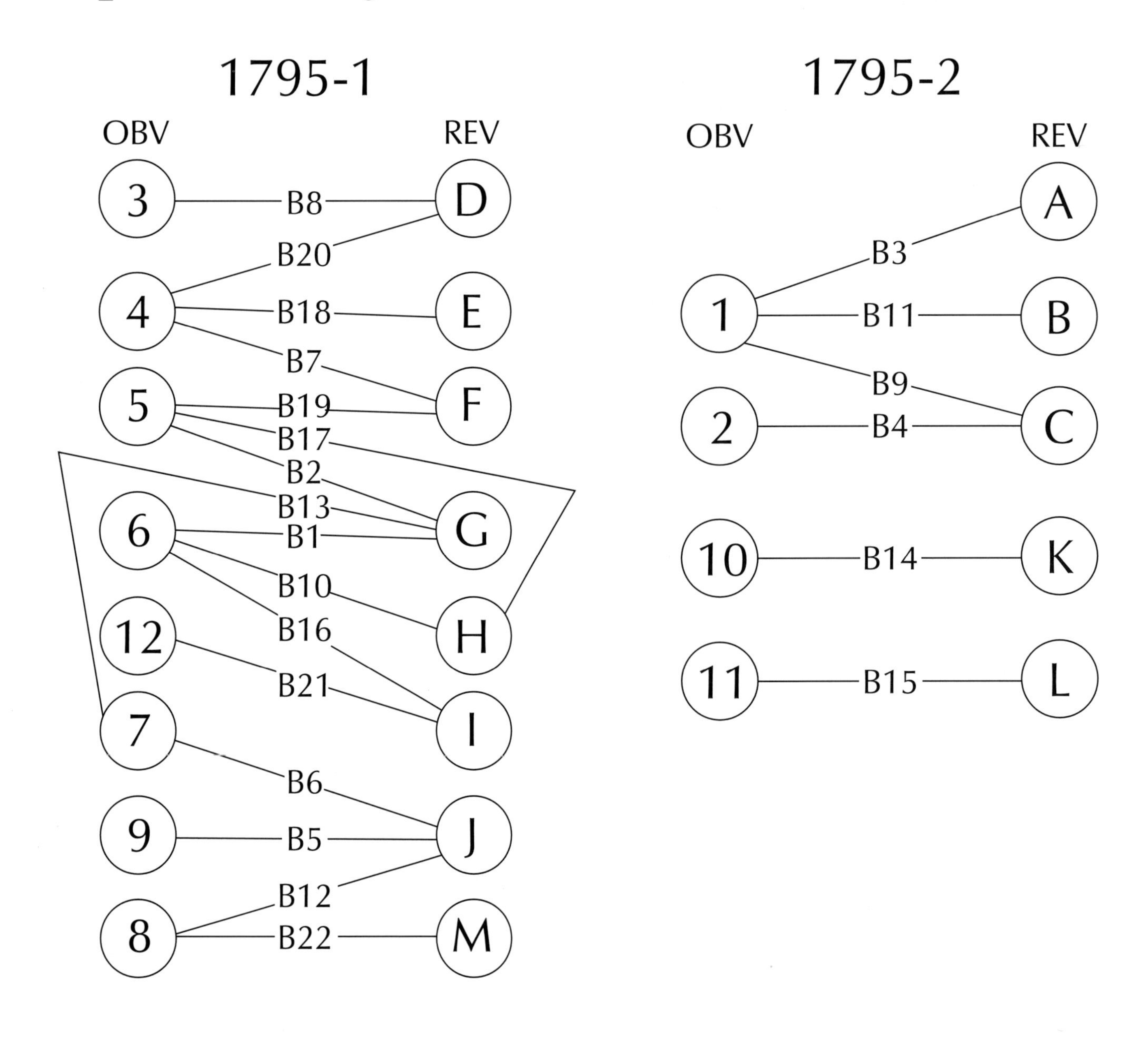

Rapid Finder for 1795 cont.

REVERSE Berries: six on left, six on right; Bolender 22; three leaves each wing.

REVERSE Berries: seven on left, six on right; Bolender 5-6-12; three leaves.
B5 Obv.—bar 2mm long down to left toward star 5.
B6 Obv.—E in LIBERTY cut over an R (weak).
B12 Obv.—lowest curl goes through the point of star 1.

REVERSE Berries: seven on left, seven on right; Bolender 7-19; three leaves.
B7 Obv.—sharp line near head connects lower two curls.
B19 Obv.—lowest curl is pierced by star 1.

REVERSE Berries: eight on left, eight on right; Bolender 3-2; leaves.

REVERSE Berries: eight on left, eleven on right; Bolender 18.
B18 No outer berry under A in STATES; two leaves.

REVERSE Berries: nine on left, eight on right; Bolender 4-9; two leaves.
B4 Star 15 is completely under bust.
B9 Star 15 is only partially under bust.

REVERSE Berries: nine on left, nine on right; Bolender 10-17; two leaves.
B10 Low curl touches top right point of star 1.
B17 Low curl heavy into star 1.

REVERSE Berries: nine on left, ten on right; B1, B2, B8, B11, B13, B16, B20, B21; Outer berry under right foot of A2; two leaves.
B1 Star 1 just touches lowest curl with top right point.
B2 Star 1 heavily into lowest curl, section missing.
B13 Star 1 has two points touching lowest curl.

Outer berry under left tip of A2-2; wings.
B8 Star 15 right of bust.
B20 Star 15 partly under bust.

Outer berry under center of A2-2; wings.
B11 Inner berry under left foot of A2.
B16 No inner berry under A2; Point of star 1 touches lowest curl.
B21 Same reverse as B16; lowest curl distant from stars 1 and 2.

Draped Bust; B14 and B15
B14 seven berries in left branch, three outside of wreath.
B15 six berries in left branch, two outside of wreath.

Flowing Hair Type-1795

B1

OBVERSE 6—used on **B1**, **B10**, and **B16**. The date is wide, with 1 and 7 farthest apart. A sharp line from the left side of the 7 just above the bottom runs up to the left towards the top of the 7 right of the serif of the 7. Star 1 touches the bottom of the lowest curl left of the tip of the curl. See description of **B10**.

REVERSE G—used on **B1**, **B2**, and **B13**. Two leaves under each wing. Nine berries on left and ten on right. Two berries under I1 and two under I2. Left bottom serif of R1 touches top feather of right wing centered between tip of top feather and tip of second feather.

Rarity 1

B2

OBVERSE 5—used on **B2**, **B17**, and **B19**. There are six prominent curls. The lowest curl is pierced and separated by a point of star 1. Star 8 is 2mm from L1, farther than any other variety. The date is wide, with the 95 closer than the other figures. There is a diagonal bar, the top of which is right of the inner point of star 4. The bar runs down to the right for about 2mm.

REVERSE G—used on **B1**, **B2**, and **B13**. See description of **B1**.

Rarity 1

B3

OBVERSE 1—used on **B3**, **B9**, and **B11**. Flowing hair in six curls. The third curl from the top turns down and touches the fourth curl. The lowest curl touches the two upper points of star 1. The 7 and 5 in the date were double struck. The 7 was moved to the left, and the 5 was struck lower and to the right.

REVERSE A—used only on **B3**. The only variety with sixteen berries, eight on each branch. Two leaves under each wing.

Die State: a: Early

Die State: b: Reverse crack rim to lower serif of C1 towards third feather up to right wing of eagle.

Rarity 5

B4

OBVERSE 2—used only on **B4**. Star 1 is closer to the 1 in the date than on any other 1795 variety, about 1-1/2 mm. Star 15 is completely under the bust. There is a small lump touching the underside of the chin.

REVERSE C—used on **B4** and **B9**; seventeen berries: nine on left branch, eight on right. A berry on the outside of the wreath between S and T of STATES. There is a short heavy crack from the outer berry under the right tip of A1 toward the left side of the upright of T3.

Rarity 3

B5

OBVERSE 9—Used only on **B5**; a very common variety. Six curls on hair, the third and fourth close together. A bar over 2mm long from very close to the upper curl down to the left toward star 5.

REVERSE J—used on **B5**, **B6** and **B12**. Thirteen berries, seven on left branch, six on right. Three leaves under each wing of eagle. All examples seen of **B5** and **B6** have a small crack down from the end of the left stem, but not on **B12**.

Rarity 1

Die State a: As described.

Die State b: Many heavy scratches up to the right from top of date to bottom of bust, with others, also up to the right, from top of neck. A blob appears around star 3 and up to the right.

B6

OBVERSE 7—used on **B6** and **B13**. **B13** has a very short foot on R in LIBERTY. **B6** has been reported with the same short foot, but is usually seen on later die states of **B6** with the foot of R which has been extended and is longer than usual. It would seem that **B13** was struck first, then **B6** with the short foot on R, then a later die state of **B6** with the longer foot at R. E in LIBERTY has been cut over an R. The R is very weak, but can be seen. The 1 and 7 are the farthest apart, the 9 and 5 next, and the 7 and 9 closest.

REVERSE J—used on **B5**, **B6** and **B12**., There are seven berries on the left branch, and six on the right. There are three leaves under each wing. A tiny sharp crack extends from the tip of the left stem.

Die State a: Foot of R in LIBERTY is short, having been made with a broken punch.

Die State b: The die has been lapped, shortening all of the curls. The lowest curl ends between two upper points of the first star. The foot of R in LIBERTY has been lengthened with an engraving tool, and now has an awkward irregular look.

Rarities: Die State a, R7; Die State b, R3

B7

OBVERSE 4—used on **B7**, **B18**, and **B20**. The lowest curl almost completes a loop, and a point of star 1 just touches the loop. A short, sharp line which just touches the hair connects the lowest curl to the one above. The E in LIBERTY is somewhat high.

REVERSE F—used on **B7** and **B19**. Seven berries on each branch, the only fourteen berry reverse. Between the left wing and the bow, there is only one berry inside the wreath, and none outside. Three leaves under each wing.

Rarity 4

B8

OBVERSE 3—**B8** is the only variety using this obverse die. The lowest curl almost makes a complete circle. The center top point of star 1 just touches the bottom of the lowest curl. The last star is farther from the 5 than any other variety of 1795. The head is not well centered. It is too high and too far to the left.

REVERSE D—used on **B8** and **B20**. The berry outside the wreath and under the left stand of A2, and the berry inside of the wreath and under the right stand of A2 show that this die is different from all of the other nineteen berry varieties. There are two leaves under each wing. Obverse crack from R down toward 7, most obvious at eye area.

Rarity 6

B9

OBVERSE 1—used on **B3**, **B9**, and **B11**. See obverse description in **B3**. The only difference between **B3** and **B9** is that **B9** has quite heavy clash marks, while **B3** and **B11** have none. It seems that **B9** was the last of the three struck.

REVERSE C—used on **B4** and **B9**. The heavy crack from the berry under the right tip of A1 toward the left side of the upright of T2 is on both **B4** and **B9**, but there are no clash marks on **B4** as there are on **B9**. See reverse description of **B4**.

Rarity 3

B10

OBVERSE 6—used on **B1**, **B10**, and **B16**. See description of **B1**. The obverses of the three varieties all seem to be alike, with one exception. The 7 in the date seems to be different on each of the three varieties. On **B1** the upright of the 7 is wedge-shaped, much thicker at the bottom. On the other two the upright of the 7 is much thinner, probably after having been reworked. On **B1** there is a very heavy line pointed straight up. This line looks like there was a 1 punched in by mistake. There is a tiny lump near the bottom of the right side of the 7 which looks like the bottom serif of a 1. On **B10** there is a bent line, much weaker than the vertical line on **B1**. On **B16** there is a very thin line touching the left side of the upright of the 7. The rest of the features on the obverses seem to be alike, so the 7 was probably reworked. On **B10** and **B16** the top of the 7 looks like it was added.

REVERSE H—used on **B10** and **B17**. Eighteen berries, nine on left branch, nine on right. Two berries in wreath on each side. Between the upper berry inside of the right wing and the wing, there seems to be a small group of stems which may have held a berry, because Bolender says that the reverse has nineteen berries. Under the tip of the leaf on the left over the head of the eagle there is only a small point remaining from a leaf.

Rarity 7

B11

OBVERSE 1—used on **B3**, **B9**, and **B11**. See obverse description in **B3**. As on **B3**, there are no clash marks. **B9** has heavy clash marks.

REVERSE B—used only on **B11**. Nineteen berries, nine on left, ten on right. Two berries in wreath under A1, the upper having a fine line halfway toward the right tip of A. Only one berry under OF, under O on the inside of the wreath. Two berries under S1, one inside and one outside of the wreath. Two more under A2. Two leaves under each wing.

Rarity 6

B12

OBVERSE 8—used on **B12** and **B22**. The lowest curl goes through the point of star 1. The curl continues to the right, ending in a sharp point over the right point of star 1. Wide date, with less space between 7 and 9, than between the others. There is more space between I and B in LIBERTY than between the other letters.

REVERSE J—used on **B5**, **B6**, and **B12**. There is no crack from the tip of the left stem. See reverse of **B5**.

Die State a: Obverse perfect.

Die State b: Faint crack from top of 7 to bust near curl.

Die State c: Crack is very heavy, extending to the rim below, and to level with the second hair curl from the top. The obverse is now in two levels, higher to the right of the crack. A heavy lump to the right about one third from the bottom of the 7 connects the crack to the 7.

Rarity 5

B13

OBVERSE 7—used on **B6** and **B13**. See description of **B6**. It seems that **B13** was struck before **B6**. The E in LIBERTY is struck over an R, and all of the letters on **B13** show double strikes and extra lines. Most of these are gone by the time the lengthened foot of R turned up on **B6**, but the R under E is still seen, although it is very weak.

REVERSE G—used on **B1**, **B2** and **B13**. See description of **B1**. Looking for unusual marks for identification, on **B13** there is a strong line up from the left tip of the serif of F in OF, parallel to the upright of F. It ends even with the crossbar of F with a little U connected at the top. There are signs of this line on **B2**, and they are practically gone on **B1**. It looks like **B13** was the first use of the reverse die, **B2** the second use, and **B1** the third.

Rarity 3

B14—DRAPED BUST, SMALL EAGLE REVERSE

OBVERSE 10—**B14** only**.** Drapery around bust, ribbon bow at back of hair. The figure is not centered, but is placed too far left. The high wave of the curl is under the center of B in LIBERTY, and the first star touches the second curl from the bottom.

REVERSE K—The small eagle is used, with seven berries in the left branch, four inside and three outside. There is an extra tip just above and slightly right of the palm leaf closest to the right wing.

Rarity 3

B15—DRAPED BUST, SMALL EAGLE REVERSE

OBVERSE 11—**B15** only. Drapery and ribbon are like **B14**, but the figure is well centered. The high wave of the curl is under the upright of E, and the first star is distant from the lowest curl.

REVERSE L—The small eagle is used with six berries in the left branch, four inside and two outside. There is a crack from the left touching the first S in STATES and the leaves under STAT. There is a heavy point under the back of the eagle's mouth. There are several blobs in the palm leaves under F.

Rarity 2

B16—FLOWING HAIR TYPE

OBVERSE 6, used on **B1**, **B10**, and **B16.** See description in **B1**. From the marks in the 1 of the date, it seems that **B1** was struck first, **B10** second, and **B16** third.

REVERSE I—new, used on **B16** and **B21**. Nineteen berries, nine on left, ten on right. Outer berry under left upright of N1 and an outer berry under center of A2. A berry on the inside of wreath under center of M1. No outer berry under either I. Point of 3rd outer leaf on right is under center of I2.

Rarity 8

B17
OBVERSE 5—used on **B2**, **B17**, and **B19**. See description of **B2**.

REVERSE H—used on **B10** and **B17**. See description of **B10**.
This variety was sold in Bolender's 79th sale, Nov. 29, 1932, Lot 220. It was first called **B20**, then changed to **B19**. It is not believed to exist.

Rarity 8

B18
OBVERSE 4—used on **B7**, **B18**, and **B20**. See description of **B7**.

REVERSE E—used only on **B18**. This reverse die has two leaves under each wing, and eleven berries on the right branch. There is no outer berry under A1.
Note: This coin was sold as Lot 2168 in the Louis E. Eliasberg, Sr. Collection by Bowers & Merena and Stack's.

Rarity 8

B19
OBVERSE 5—used on **B2** and **B19**. See description of **B2**. This variety was first called **B20**, later changed to **B19**.

REVERSE F—used on **B7** and **B19**. See description of **B7**. One of our experts has seen a picture of this, so it probably exists. Any information will be welcomed.

Rarity 8

B20
OBVERSE 4—used on **B7**, **B18**, and **B20**. See description of **B7**.

REVERSE D—used on **B8** and **B20**. See description of **B8**.

Rarity 8

B21

OBVERSE 12—used only on **B21**. The lowest curl is practically a closed circle, with the point coming around more than a complete circle, but not touching anything. The circular curl is just about the same distance from two points of the star 1 and 2 points of star 2. The five upper curls all come out to the left about the same amount, more so than on any other 1795 obverse. The highest wave of the hair is under the left tip of R. The last star is distant from the bust, and points to just above the upper edge.

This is a new obverse. There are several lines, vertical and horizontal, made with a sharp instrument. It looks like the coin might have been canceled at the mint. This may not be a normal cancellation. I have another dollar, 1796 **B6**, which is almost certainly canceled. In this case a very blunt instrument was used, and the cancellation looks like spokes of a wheel. It is possible that there was no standard method. Of course, it is possible that either this coin or my 1796 **B6** was not canceled, and maybe some day some better evidence will turn up.

The coin mentioned above was sold by Spink America as Lot 186, on June 3, 1997. The hammer price was approx. $21,000 plus commission. Before the sale, representatives of Spink America brought the coin to Wilmington for an opinion as to its authenticity. When we discovered that it had the same reverse as my **B16**, and the coin checked out from every angle, the opinion was that it was real.

Rarity 8

B22

OBVERSE 8—used on **B12** and **B22**. See description of **B12**. This coin was probably struck before the two **B12**s in my collection, because both of the **B12**s have cracks through the 7 in the date, while the **B22** is not cracked.

REVERSE M—has not been seen on any other 1795 variety. It is the only 1795 variety with six berries on the left side and six on the right.

Rarity 8

Chapter Three:

Rapid Finder for 1796

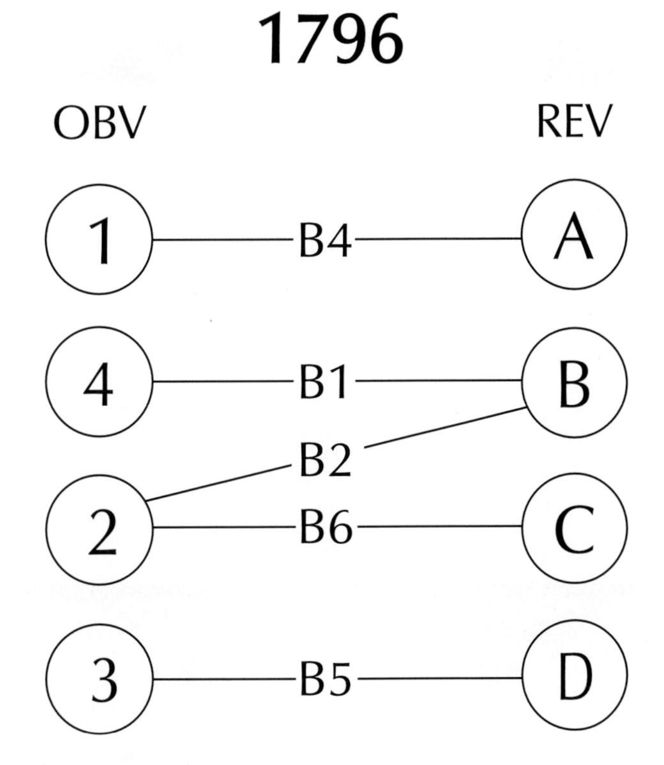

REVERSE Berries: seven on left, none on right. B1, B2, B5.

B1 Two points of star 1 touch lowest curl.

B2 One point of star 1 touches lowest curl.

B5 Large lump at right top of A2.

REVERSE Berries: eight on left, none on right; B4, B6.

B4 No heavy vertical crack on reverse.

B6 Heavy vertical crack from rim to rim, touches O1 and C1.

Note: There is no B3

B1 DRAPED BUST, SMALL EAGLE 1796

OBVERSE 4—used on **B1**. Small date, 7 and 9 farthest apart, 9 and 6 are closest. Two points of star 1 touch lowest curl.

REVERSE B—used on 1795 **B14**, 1796 **B1**, **B2**, 1797 **B2**, and 1798 **B2**.

The small eagle is used, with seven berries in the left branch, four inside and three outside. There is an extra tip just above and slightly right of the palm leaf closest to the right wing. A line from the right side of this tip is fairly strong.

Rarity 4

B2

OBVERSE 2—used on **B2** and **B6**. Small wide date, a point of a curl comes out between the two lowest curls and is just touched by the upper point of star. A spike from the curl which comes out between the two lowest curls runs from this curl to the third curl from the bottom.

REVERSE B—used on 1795 **B14**, 1796 **B1** and **B2**, 1797 **B2**, and 1798 **B2**. The extra tip of a leaf mentioned in **B1** is not present on **B2**, even though the **B2** is a higher grade coin.

Rarity 4

B3

Note: This coin has been a problem for many years. It has been advertised again and again, in coin papers and auction catalogs. Most of the recent writings about it, including mine, question its existence. When I mentioned it in a previous edition of Bolender, one dealer told me (humorously, I hope) that he was going to put out a "hit" on me.

Now I am going to stick my neck out. I am saying that it does not exist. Here is why: I had been looking for this variety for many years, having ordered them from ads, only to return them as being attributed incorrectly. I looked for this variety at many coin shows, with no success. I finally found one at a F.U.N. Show in Florida. Here it was, with a large dot over the 1 in the date, and a small letter reverse. I couldn't write the check for $1000 fast enough.

I told the dealer that I wanted to check it out a little better, and would return it shortly if it proved to be not the one I wanted. It was not attributed, but it was one variety which I knew by heart. I walked the floor until I found a dealer with a copy of Bolender, which he graciously loaned. As soon as things were compared, it was plain to see that it had the wrong obverse. The high wave of the hair was not correct, and many other little things. The large dot over the 1 was there. I had seen it. I looked at it under a strong light, with a 7 power B & L glass. It had a hole in it, showing that it had been made with a sharp instrument. When I looked at it the first time, I had seen the lump, but had not noticed the hole.

I returned the coin to the dealer, who gave back my check. In thinking it over, could this have been the coin that the discoverer of **B3** had seen, or did someone make it just to have one. Unless someone comes forth with the truth, we may never know. In any event, I've stuck out my head, so chop it off if you find a real one.

B4

OBVERSE 1—used only on **B4**. Star 1 does not touch lowest curl, but two points of it almost touch the curl. There is a small vertical line between the two lower points of star 11, and a couple of lines in the lower half of star 13. There is a heavy dot over the 1 in the date, which gradually grows smaller with use of the die. The R in LIBERTY has a long pointed foot, with the toe pointed downward.

REVERSE A—used only on **B4**. There are eight berries on the left side of the wreath, with three outside, and five inside the wreath.

Rarity 2

Die State a: Lump over 1 is very heavy, shaped like a football.
Die State b: Lump over 1 is small, like a dot.
Die State c: Lump over 1 is practically gone, only a tiny trace remains.

B5

OBVERSE 3—used only on **B5**. The top of the 6 in the date is heavily doubled. The top point of star 1 and the tip of the serif of the 1 in the date both almost touch the curls. The stars on the left side are spaced apart, but on **B1**, **B2**, **B5** and **B6** the stars on the right side almost touch each other. On **B4** the stars on the right side are rather far apart.

REVERSE D—used only on **B5**. There are seven large berries in the wreath, with what might be a tiny eighth berry on the stem of the lowest sprig of leaves on the inside of the wreath. This reverse is different from the others, with several leaves touching letters in the legend.

Rarity 4

Die State a: A small lump appears to the right of I2, but does not touch .

Die State b: The lump grows larger, now touching I2, covering the right top serif. Other lumps appear inside the tops of A1 and A2, over the left side of E3. The right bottom serif of E3 is now a large irregular mass.

Die State c: The lump is now monstrous, covering part of the top of I2. (Queller)

B6

OBVERSE 2—used on **B2** and **B6**-See description of **B2**.

REVERSE C—used only on **B6**-Lowest outer berry is between N1 and I1.

Four berries inside the wreath, four outside. A heavy vertical die break from rim to rim touches left side of O1 down through the center of C1, where it turns left past A3 to the dentils. This is a very interesting break, because the 20% of the coin to the right of the break is strongly struck, appearing to be at least two grades higher than the rest of the coin, which is weakly struck.

Note: This variety is quite rare at the time this is written. Only two examples are known. On the one photographed here, the obverse has been canceled with radial lines. We think that this was done at the mint and that the dies were not used again.

Rarity 8

Chapter Four:

Rapid Finder for 1797

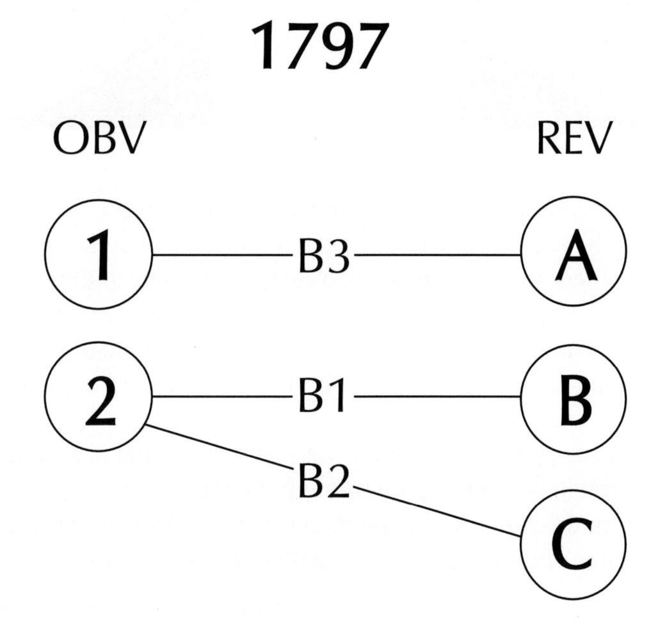

OBVERSE Stars: nine on left, seven on right**; B1**, **B2**

REVERSE Berries: eight on left, **B1**; seven on left, **B2**

OBVERSE Stars: ten on left, six on right**; B3**

B1

OBVERSE 2—used on **B1** and **B2**. Sixteen stars, nine on left, seven on right. 179 in date are fairly level with each other, but the second 7 is quite high. It was very difficult to get all sixteen stars on the die, and they either touch the adjacent one or are very close to it. There is a football shaped lump under star 9, the top left star.

REVERSE C—used only on **B1**. Three berries outside of the wreath, five inside. The lowest inside berry is between the bow and the lowest inside leaf. The tops of all three Es on the reverse have lumps in them, made with a damaged E punch. E2 was double punched.

Die State a: Obverse and reverse are perfect, except for the minor items mentioned above.

Die State b: Obverse cracked through 97, curving up through the bust.

Die State c: Obverse cracked from the rim through the 9, curving left through the curls.

Die State d: The obverse die is now completely cracked, with over twenty cracks.

Rarity 3

B2

OBVERSE 2—used on **B1** and **B2**. Nine stars on left, seven on right. 179 fairly level, last 7 high.

REVERSE C—used on 1795 **B14**, 1796 **B1**, 1796 **B2**, 1797 **B2**, and 1798 **B2**. The extra tip just above and slightly right of the palm leaf closest to the right wing is very strong.

Rarity 4

B3

OBVERSE 1—Sixteen stars, ten left and six right. The date resembles obverse die 2, with the second 7 higher than the first three numbers, but it is the only 1797 with only six stars on the right. The high wave of the hair is completely under the E, but on the other two varieties it is under the left side of the upright, with half of the curl left of the E.

REVERSE A—The lowest berry on the reverse is on the outside of the wreath, but on **B1** and **B2** the lowest berry is on the inside of the wreath.

Rarity 2

Die State a: Large planchet, struck with a collar of a slightly larger diameter.
Die State b: Small planchet, slightly less in diameter, but slightly thicker.

Chapter Five:

Rapid Finder for 1798 Small Eagle Reverse

1798-1

OBV		REV	
1	B2	A	SM ALL
2	B1	B	SM ALL
	B32		
3	B4	C	
	B5		
	B3	D	
4	B20		
	B7	E	
5	B6		
	B17		
6		F	
	B18		
7	B22	G	
	B23		
8	B19	H	
	B21		
9	B13	I	
	B10		
		J	

1798-2

OBV		REV
10	B16	K
	B11	
11	B15	L
	B27	
12	B26	M
	B31	
13	B30	N
	B33	
14	B28	O
	B29	
15	B12	P
16	B9	Q
17	B14	R
18	B25	S
	B24	T
19	B8	U

B1 **OBVERSE** 2—has thirteen stars; **REVERSE** B
B2 **OBVERSE** 1—has fifteen stars; **REVERSE** A

Heraldic Eagle Reverse

USED ON ALL SILVER DOLLARS THROUGH 1804
SEE APPENDIX A FOR LOCATION NUMBERS

Appendix No.	Bolender No.	Description
1223	B9	**REVERSE** R—a berry is under the left serif of A3.
1234	B11, B15, B16, B27	**REVERSE** K—third berry is tiny, and attached to the point of the largest leaf on the right.
	B11	**OBVERSE** 11—bottom of lowest curl is very weak.
	B15	**OBVERSE** 12—the point of star 7 is above the bottom of L, and very close—1mm.
	B16	**OBVERSE** 10—heavy crack from the rim under star 1 to the lowest curl-to the tops of 179.
	B27	**OBVERSE** 13—defect under inner point of star 12, toward throat.
1324	B3, B7, B20	**REVERSE** E—stem of branch curves outward.
	B3	**OBVERSE** 3—two heavy dots on bust, three tiny dots under E.
	B7	**OBVERSE** 4—a heavy line-up to the right, 2mm right of 8.
	B20	**OBVERSE** 6—a crack up from 7 in date, ends in lump over 9.
1336	B18, B22	**REVERSE** G—right serifs of Ts are longer than left serifs.
	B18	**OBVERSE** 6—crack up from 7 in date ends in a lump over 9.
	B22	**OBVERSE** 7—line down to the right from left side of lowest curl.
1434	B13, B21	**REVERSE** I—second star from left touches cloud 3, a tiny cloud under A1, and is the only star to touch a cloud on reverse 1.
	B13	**OBVERSE** 9—a string of tiny lumps up along right side of L.
	B21	**OBVERSE** 6—a heavy football-shaped lump over left side of 9.
1445	B19, B23	**REVERSE** H—heavy lumps between T and E in STATES
	B19	**OBVERSE** 8—a heavy crack from the bottom of E runs down into the hair. The die section to the left of this crack rises.
	B23	**OBVERSE** 7—8 in the date is firmly connected to bottom of bust
1546	B10	**REVERSE** J—lumps around bottom of stem.
	B10	**OBVERSE** 9—heavy line up along right side of L.
1556	B28	**REVERSE** P—lumps inside of M, between E and R, and I and C.
	B28	**OBVERSE** 13—used on 7 varieties. 3 heavy cracks under date.
2546	B5	**REVERSE** D—heavy vertical crack through right side of shield.
	B5	**OBVERSE** 3—two strong dots under E.
3335	B30	**REVERSE** N—huge lump on A2, on late die state.
	B30	**OBVERSE** 13—used on seven varieties, three heavy cracks under date.

Appendix No.	Bolender No.	Description
3435	B14	**REVERSE** S—many lumps in E1.
	B14	**OBVERSE** 16—heavy crack inside of stars 1-5.
3545	B24, B25	**REVERSE** T—three left arrow points missing. Many heavy lumps around stars, and at bottom of stem.
	B24	**OBVERSE** 18—L-I-B spaced far apart.
	B25	**OBVERSE** 17—LIB very close to each other.
3546	B26	**REVERSE** L—Several cracks through T2, T3, E2, and S2.
	B26	**OBVERSE** 13—used on seven varieties, three cracks under date are weak.
3546	B31	**REVERSE** M—three upper berries are tiny, and have no stems.
	B31	**OBVERSE** 13—used on seven varieties, three cracks are weak. Spikes up from tops of LIBERTY.
3546	B33	**REVERSE** O—defect across reverse from rim over right side of T1-rim over left side of M. Cracks on both ends, and a raised section between.
4435	B4, B32	**REVERSE** C-reverse stars are arranged in straight lines, tent like.
	B4	**OBVERSE** 3—two strong dots under E.
	B32	**OBVERSE** 2—thirteen stars.
4545	B6, B17	**REVERSE** F—a heavy crack from the center between the tops of R and I-runs up to the right to the dentils over I.
	B6	**OBVERSE** 4—a short crack runs up to the right-right of 8.
	B17	**OBVERSE** 5—many strong lumps from star 1 through the date, to the right of the 8.
5546	B8	**REVERSE** U—many cracks on the reverse, around the entire reverse. Most of UNITED is gone, as is part of C.
	B8	**OBVERSE** 19—star 5 is missing, as are most of stars 4 and 7.
5556	B12, B29	**REVERSE** Q—star 12 is connected to the lower beak.
	B12	**OBVERSE** 14—many cracks, between 7 and 9, through 9, etc./top of 8 is doubled to the left.
	B29	**OBVERSE** 13—used on seven varieties. The three cracks are quite heavy.

1798 Draped Bust Obverse-Small Eagle Reverse

B1
OBVERSE 2—thirteen stars, only 1798 Small eagle obverse with thirteen stars.

REVERSE B—used for 1797 **B1**, three berries outside of the wreath, five berries inside. The lowest berry is between the bow and the lowest inside leaf.

Rarity 2
Die State a: Reverse crack from rim through upright of T3 to leaf below. Another crack from rim over A1 down through top of T3-E2, S2 right wreath.
Die State b: Reverse cracks in State a, plus crack from rim to N1, wreath left wing near top, leaves under A1. Another crack near dentils from over D1 to over T2. Another crack down through ED up through ST. Another crack from tops of OF down through AMERI.

B2
OBVERSE 1-15 stars—only 1798 Small eagle obverse with fifteen stars.

REVERSE A—used on 1795 **B14**, 1796 **B1**, **B2**, 1797 **B2**. Three berries outside of the wreath, four inside.

Rarity 2

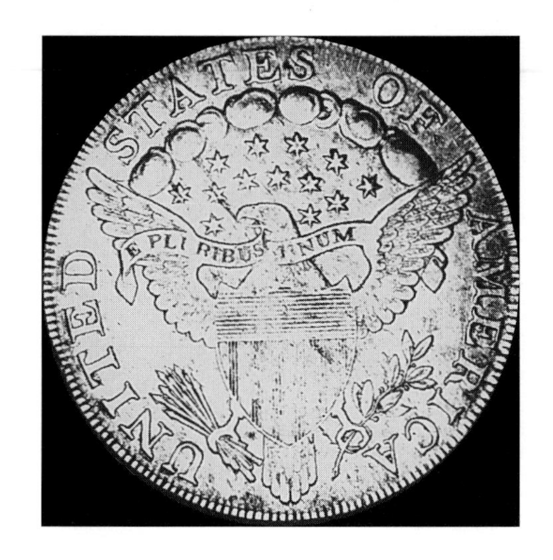

1798 13-Star Obverses-Heraldic Eagle Reverses

B3

OBVERSE 3—used on **B3**, **B4**, and **B5**. Star 7 is close to L, but star 8 is distant from Y. There are two dots on the bust, very close to the drapery. There is one dot in a furrow in the hair even with the throat, and two dots under the E in LIBERTY.

REVERSE E-1, 3, 2, 4—used on **B3**, **B7**, and **B20**. Star is distant from eagle's beak. Leaf at I2 is left of serif of I. Stem of branch curves outward.

Rarity 5

B4

OBVERSE 3—used on **B3**, **B4**, and **B5**. See description of **B3**.

REVERSE C-4, 4, 3, 5—used on **B4** and **B32**. Third arrow from left has a very weak arrowhead, third arrow from right has no arrowhead. Point of star 12 is just inside of eagle's beak. While most of the eagle's claw under A3 have one sharp point on the left toe and one on the right toe, reverse C has two points on the right toe.

Rarity 3

B5

OBVERSE 3—used on **B3**, **B4**, and **B5**. See description of **B3**.

REVERSE D-2, 5, 4, 6—used only on **B5**. Thirteen arrowheads, but only seven shafts. There are two arrowheads each on three of the shafts, with the other three arrowheads without shafts. The top of F1 is missing, but the right top serif is strong, floating by itself. A very heavy slightly curved crack runs from right of S2—just right of M in UNUM—touches the right side of the shield-through the right claw to the rim under the right side of the tail. The reverse is in two levels, much stronger on the right side of the crack. Another crack very close to S2 helps a cud to appear just right of S2. Another cud, heavier, runs just outside the shield from the top of the horizontal lines to the rim under the tail feathers. There are some heavy lumps inside the shield, the largest on the right side of the fourth group.

Note: Haseltine and Bolender had seen but a single example of this variety. It was owned by Col. Green, Bolender, Austin, Ostheimer, and Reiver. This is the coin in the above photograph.

Rarity 6

B6

OBVERSE 4—used on **B6** and **B7**. The tip of the 1 would almost touch the lowest curl if it was complete. The 8 almost touches the bottom of the bust.

There is a strong line, up slightly to the right, right of the lower loop of 8.

REVERSE F-4, 5, 4, 5—used on **B6** and **B17**. There are ten arrowheads, on nine shafts. Three shafts have two arrowheads each, and two shafts have no arrowheads.

Die State a: Obverse and reverse as described.

Die State b: Crack develops from star 1 down to near the dentils under the lowest curl-up through the 798 of the date.

Die State c: The crack in state b is now heavy, with a branch up to the lowest curl. An elongated lump appears in the crack near star 1. The crack continues up through star 1, curving to the right to the lowest ribbon. A branch of this crack breaks off to go through stars 6 and 7. On the reverse, the two arrow shafts without arrowheads have been removed. This is the way the die was used on **B17**.

Rarity 2

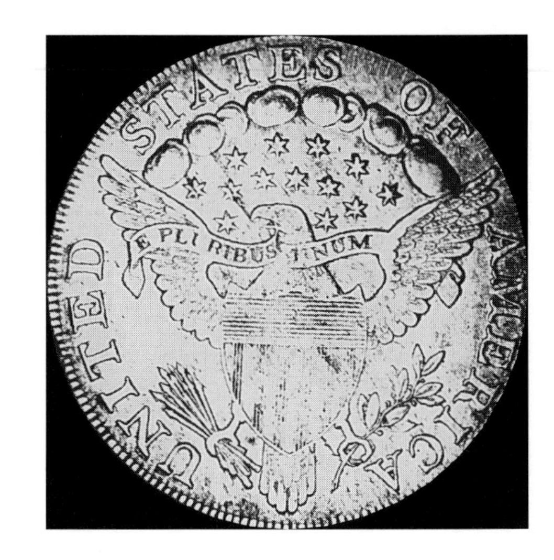

B7

OBVERSE 4—used on **B6** and **B7**. See description of **B6**. **B7** might have been struck before **B6**.

REVERSE E-1, 3, 2, 4—used on **B3**, **B7**, and **B20**. See description of **B3**. There is a curved clash mark through F.

Rarity 5

B8

OBVERSE 19—used only on **B8**. Thirteen stars, all nice and strong. There is a heavy, blunt vertical line in the field between stars 2 and 3 and the hair. There is a tiny crack from the right side of E in LIBERTY to the hair below. There are many dots between the front of the head and the stars to right, in front of the neck, and around the coin in general. Thirteen full stars, seven on the left and six on the right.

REVERSE U-5, 5, 4, 6—used only on **B8**. There is a fine crack through the top of UNITED to the left wing-to the top of S1. A heavy crack from the rim over T3 touches the left top serif of E2. Crack runs from the center of the right foot of M1 down to the left almost to the ribbon, and up slightly to the right.

Note: Several years ago an article in *The Numismatist* told of a new discovery of a 1798 dollar having only twelve stars. I started looking for it, and finally found one. When I checked it, there were only eleven stars. I kept looking, and now have what I call the **B8** with thirteen stars, twelve, eleven, ten, nine, and eight stars.

Die State a: Thirteen stars on obv.; rev. legend complete

Die State b: Twelve stars, star 5 is gone; rev. bottoms of TED gone.

Die State c: Eleven stars, stars 4 and 5 are gone; rev. N, parts of U, N, I, T, E, D gone.

Die State d: Ten stars, stars 4, 5, and 7 are gone; rev. N and E are gone, and U, I, T, D are half gone. Head of eagle weak.

Die State e: Nine stars, stars 4, 5 and 7 are gone, star 3 and L are 1/2 gone; rev. N and E are gone, U, I, T, D weak Eagle gone.

Die State f: Eight stars, stars 3, 4, 5, 6, 7, and L are gone; rev. NITE gone, half of U and D left. Entire eagle and bottom row of stars gone.

Rarity 2

B9

OBVERSE 15—used only on **B9**; 8 in the date is very close to the bust, the 1, 7 and 9 are distant. The lowest curl is very weak on the right side, with the 1 in the date pointing through a hole in the curl. The coin is nicely made. The only items which can be used to identify it are two tiny dots, both close to the hair. One is under the left tip of E in LIBERTY, and the other is almost touching the hair under the left side of the upright of R.

REVERSE R-1, 2, 2, 9, used only on **B9**. Leaf under I points to just inside of the tip of the foot of R.

Rarity 4

Die State a: Obverse and reverse perfect.

Die State b: Edge through 17-bust. Edge to two lower points of star 2. Cracks from star 3 to star 6. Reverse has crack through STATES OF AM, and one down through M to ribbon.

B10

OBVERSE 9—used on **B10** and **B13**. Heavy crack up from tip of right serif of L in LIBERTY up to the rim. A light crack from the dentils under 7 in the date, under the 1 to stars 1-2-3-4-left of stars 5, 6, 7. Three or four lumps lined up between star 13 and the bust, with star 13 pointing right at the largest lump. There is a lump over the right serif of the bottom of T. A line extends to the right from the right serif of Y. There are two heavy lumps in the hair bow , and two other lumps in the field toward star 7.

REVERSE J-1, 5, 4, 6—used only on **B10**. Thirteen perfect arrows. The four shafts towards the shield have two arrowheads each, and the five shafts to the left have one arrowhead each. There is a large lump right of the tip of the stem. There is a faint crack from near the right bottom of A3 to the tip of the stem. There are many tiny lumps in the field around the stem.

Rarity 5

B11

OBVERSE 11—used only on **B11**. Heavy file marks up to the left from the top of the head and top of the bow. There is a heavy but short line in the fold of the drapery under the bust a little bit right of the center between the 8 in the date and the point of the bust.

REVERSE K, 1, 2, 3, 4—used on **B11**, **B15**, **B16**, and **B27**. The third berry from the top is tiny, and is attached to a leaf point. It looks like a berry was used to connect the center pair of leaves on the left to the stem.

Die State a: Perfect.(May be rarity 6)

Die State b: Obverse crack from rim through the lower three points of star 13 to the bust between the throat and the chin.

Die State c: A very heavy crack from the rim throughout the upper point of star 13 opposite to the crack in b, to the mouth, across the hair to a lump in the hair. Another crack goes from near this one almost to star 7. The section of the coin between the two cracks is rising.

Rarity 3

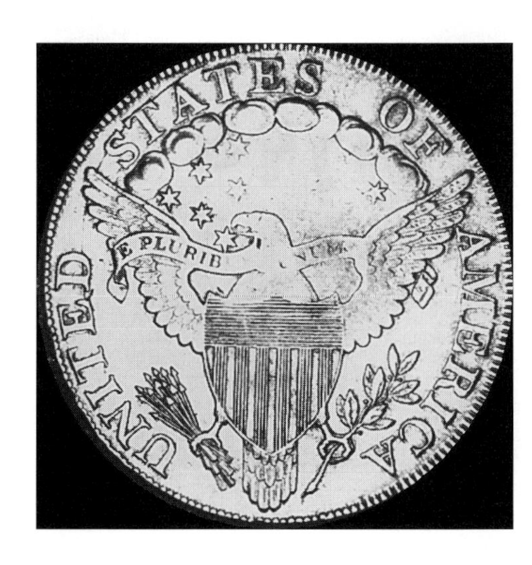

B12

OBVERSE 14—used only on **B12**. Faint lumps in upper loop of B, and between top of E and dentils. Other faint lumps are present under the foot of R and all of T. The high waves of the hair are slightly left of the center of E, and under the center of R.

REVERSE Q-5, 5, 5, 6, used on **B12** and **B29**. There are thirteen perfect arrowheads on nine perfect shafts, the four on the right side each containing two arrowheads. **B12** was struck after **B29**. I have one **B29** with all thirteen stars, with twelve of them strong, and only the center star weak. On another **B29**, three of the stars are gone completely, and four more are weak. On the reverse of **B29**, only seven stars are seen, all six on the left and the one on the extreme right, touching the cloud under F.

Die States:

OBVERSE

a: I have not seen **B12** with a perfect obverse, but, since this is the only variety using die 14, there should be some examples around with very few or even no cracks.

b:

1. Crack from the dentils under the second curl from the bottom—touches the two inside points of star 1 into the field right of star 3.
2. A branch of this crack runs from the dentils to the second curl.
3. Another crack from the dentils halfway between the first crack and the 1 in the date meets the second crack at the second curl.
4. Tiny cracks connect stars 1, 2, 3, 6, 7, 8, 9, 10, 11, 12 and 13 to the dentils.
5. Another crack from the dentils under star 13 goes from the dentils to the left side of star 13, up across the bust and through the drapery.
6. A branch of this crack runs to the left just before it touches the bust, running through the drapery to the dentils near the 8 in the date.
7. Another branch of this crack leaves it to the right just as it touches star 13, crossing star 13 to star 12.
8. A branch of this crack crosses the center of star 12—the two inner points of star 11—the one inner point of star 10, up to the left field near stars 9 and 8.
9. There is a heavy crack straight up, first closer to the 9, then closer to the 7, then to the bust.
10. A tiny crack runs to the right above the foot of the 9 to the bottom of the loop.
11. Another crack from the dentils under the 9 curves through the right side of the nine and out the center of the top of 9.

REVERSE

12. The three stars at the left are strong. The next three are weak. The next six are missing, and the one on the far right is strong.
13. A heavy crack runs from the dentils left of U, down through UNITED, the two outermost wing tips, the tops of STA, dentils over T3. The crack continues in the dentils until it reaches the rim over M.
14. Crack runs down through A2 through the left foot of M, under E.

Rarity 4

B13

OBVERSE 9—used on **B10** and **B13**. The heavy crack up on the right side of the L in LIBERTY is present, but is very weak. The line to the right from the bottom serif of Y is there. The lumps between star 13 and the bust are almost gone, but the remnants can be seen. The lines at the bottom of Y are present. The upper left point of star 8 is sharply doubled.

REVERSE I-1, 4, 3, 4—used on **B13** and **B21**. There is a small, but heavy lump on the bottom of the cloud which touches the eagle's right wing, very close to the right wing. The tip of the feather closest to the top of the same cloud has a large lump on it, almost level with the top of the cloud. Crack starts near the top of F, touches the tip of the right wing-tops of AM, over E to the dentils over the left side of R.

Rarity 3

B14

OBVERSE 16—used only on **B14**. There is a smooth lump below star 1, with some lines and marks between star 1 and the curls. There are cracks between stars 2 and 3, 3 and 4, and the largest between 4 and 5. There is a bit of graffiti around L and below B. The highest curl is centered under the upright of E.

REVERSE S-3, 4, 3, 5—used on **B14** only. Lines and dots around T1-E1. Lines up from bottom serif of S1, right of S1, top and right of T2, top of A1, left top of T3 and E2.

Die State a: As described above.

Die State b: Field of obverse under stars 1-6 becomes lower, many lumps around E1.

Die State c: Star 7 is nearly obliterated. Crack through right part of 01.

Rarity 4

B15

OBVERSE 12—used only on **B15**. Star 7 is very close to L, with a point of the star almost reaching the serif, but pointing above it.

REVERSE K-1, 2, 3, 4—used on **B11**, **B15**, **B16**, **B27**. The third berry from the top is tiny, and is attached to a leaf point.

Die State a: Larger stars.

Die State b: Dies were probably lapped, resulting in smaller stars.

Rarity: State a, R5; State b, R3.

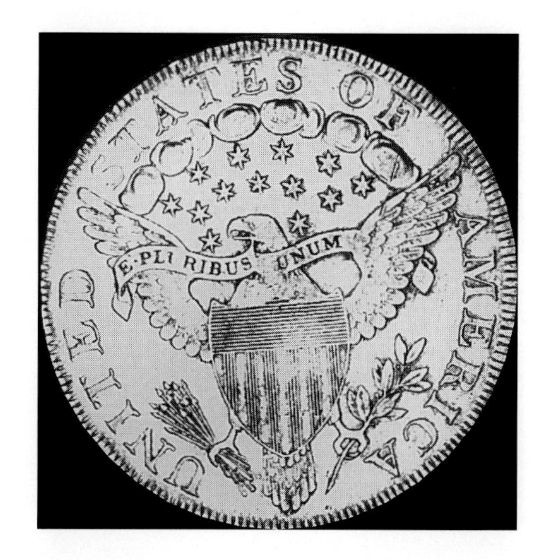

B16

OBVERSE 10—used only on **B16**. Evidently the die broke very early. There is a very heavy break from the top of the 9, just below the top of the 7, the top of the 9, the bottom of the lowest curl, the rim under star 1. The section of the crack under star 1 rises to become a cud, eliminating that portion of the crack. A tiny crack from the right of the cud runs down to the left bottom serif of 1. A tiny vertical lump appears between the top of the 1 and the serif of the 7.

REVERSE K—used on **B11**, **B15**, **B16**, and **B27**. The third berry from the top is tiny, and is attached to a leaf point.
Die State a: Obverse perfect.
Die State b: Heavy crack through top of date left to star 1.

Rarity 6

B17

OBVERSE 5—used only on **B17**. Wide date, with the top of the 8 just touching the bust. The dentils from under the 1 to the left to star 2 are long, rather thin spikes. There are many tiny lumps around the date, below the lowest curl, dentils below star 1, in star 1, right of I, below BE, and above star 9. There are elongated lumps on star 1, between star 4 and 5, down from bottom of E, and between the upper lip and star 10. There is a crack through the date-stars 1 to 4, and to the rim near stars 5 and 6.

REVERSE F-4, 5, 4, 5—used on **B6** and **B17**. **B17** was struck after the final state of **B6**. The reverse die of **B6** was lapped as it was used. The berries became smaller and smaller. **B17** starts where **B6** finishes, and as striking continues, on **B17**c the upper two berries disappear, and the three left have no stems.

Die State a: Very light crack through date, stars 1-4,outside of stars 5 and 6.

Die State b: A second crack through the dentils causes raised area from star 1 to star 4. Crack from rim to star 1 to curl.

Die State c: A heavy break from end of crack in state b causes heavy crack from star 4 to star 5, and a lighter crack to star 7. Crack mentioned in state b is very heavy, with the field higher on the right side.

Rarity 5

B18

OBVERSE 6—used on **B18**, **B20**, **B21**. There is a heavy crack from over the 7—slightly left of center—up to the right, ending in a football-shaped lump which ends almost over the inner curve of the 9. This lump also appears on both **B20** and **B21**.

REVERSE G-1, 3, 3, 5—used on **B18** and **B22**. Everything that is seen on the reverse of **B18** is exactly the same as that on **B22**, so they probably were struck by the same reverse die. **B18** has a perfect reverse, but **B22** has many cracks and breaks, so **B18** was probably struck before **B22**.

Rarity 6

B19

OBVERSE 8—used only on **B19**. Crack runs from the bottom of E in LIBERTY, under the left side of the upright of E, straight down into the hair about 5mm. The die sinks to the left of the crack, raising and dulling the hair. To the right of the crack the hair is sharp.

REVERSE H-1, 4, 4, 5—used on **B19** and **B23**. There are thirteen arrowheads on nine shafts, the four on the right having two arrowheads apiece. From the left, arrowhead 1 has no left side, number 3 is a blob, and the upper arrowhead on the third shaft from the right is gone. There is a sharp crack from the top left corner of the shield to the inside of the wing under R. The top of the reverse die was not smooth, and there are several high spots, including a sharp lump between T and E in STATES, small lumps on and right of the cloud under E and around S. There is a little crack from the top of a dentil to the top of E2 over the right side of the upright. There are heavy lumps under the cloud under S.

Die State a: As described above.

Die State b: The crack mentioned above continues down through the 1 to the border.

Rarity 4

B20

OBVERSE 6—used on **B18**, **B20**, **B21**. See description of **B18**.

REVERSE E-1, 3, 2, 4—used on **B3**, **B7**, and **B20**. Star is distant from eagle's beak. Leaf at I2 is left of serif of 1. Stem of branch curves outward. On **B20** a heavy crack from the rim over the right side of I2 runs up to the 1798 ribbon under the right wing. A branch of this crack goes to the right upper leaf. Another crack goes from the bottom of R down under E3. Also on **B20** there is a rim break through the dentils under the tail feathers and to the right on all die states seen. On **B7** and **B20** there are curved clash marks through O and F.

Die State a: Reverse, crack through I fairly light.

Die State b: Reverse, crack through I fairly heavy, part level with top of I.

Die State c: Reverse, cracks to I very heavy. Another heavy crack to toe of R, and a third, a heavy horizontal crack connects upright and foot of R.

Rarity 4

B21

OBVERSE 6—used on **B18**, **B20**, and **B21**. The heavy crack over the 7, ending with the football-shaped lump mentioned in **B18**, is present. A faint horizontal crack runs from the left side of E almost to the Y.

REVERSE I-1, 4, 3, 4—used on **B13** and **B21**. There are ten arrowheads on eight shafts. The third shaft from the right has no arrowheads. The small lump mentioned on the bottom of the cloud touching the right wing is present. The crack through the tops of AM over ER is present, but very weak.

Rarity 5

B22

OBVERSE 7—used on **B22** and **B23**, 8 firmly connected with bust. Several lines, up to the right, inside lowest curl. One line, down to the right, from the left side of curl 1.

REVERSE G-1, 3, 3, 5, used on **B18** and **B22**. There are five strong berries. The center one—third from the top or the bottom—is impaled on the tip of a leaf. Crack from the lowest star, closest to the back of the eagle's head, under the scroll, to the center of the eagle's back, between the scroll and the shield.

Die State a: Obverse perfect. Reverse cracked back of the eagle's head as mentioned above. There is a spike on the bottom of the loop of 9.

Die State b: Obverse cracked left side of bottom serif of Y-under stars 8 and 9. An incused row of dentils appears inside of the dentils—almost touching the bust—from star 12 around to the left to under the 8. There are tiny cracks up to the right from the peak of the 1, the left side of the top of the 9, and the bottom of the 8. There is a vertical crack on the right side of 1, and a tiny horizontal crack in the upper loop of 8.

Rarity 4

B23

OBVERSE 7—used on **B22** and **B23**. See description of **B22**.

REVERSE H-1, 4, 4, 5—used on **B19** and **B23**. See description of **B19**.

Die State a: On the obverse, all of the curls are strong.

Die State b: The second curl from the bottom is very weak.

Rarity 3

B24

OBVERSE 18—used only on **B24**. In the date, 7 and 9 are slightly higher than the 1. The 8 is quite a bit higher than the 7 and 9. A faint crack from the lowest curl is above the 1 to the top of the serif of 7—through the 9 just below the top—through the center of the upper loop of 8—to the dentils near the front of the bust. A fine crack runs from star 1 to under the 1 in the date. Three medium strong cracks run slightly up to the left from the dentils right of 8. One goes through the right side of the 8 and two are farther left. A heavy crack from the junction of the neck and bust curves through star 12 to the dentils. A fine crack from this crack just between star 12 and the dentils to the dentils at star 13. A fine crack goes from the center of stars 8, 9, 10, 11, 12, and 13 to the bust close to a heavy blob on the bust near the drapery.

REVERSE T-3, 5, 4, 5—used on **B24** and **B25** and on 1799 **B-15**. The six stars on the left and three stars on the bottom right are all strong, and the other 4 are weak. A heavy clash mark curves through OF. There are lines through the stars on the right. Near the point at the bottom of the stem, a very heavy break goes straight down across the dentils to the rim.

Die State a: The reverse is as described above.

Die State b: The reverse die has been lapped and the clash marks are gone. The four weak stars are gone also. The heavy break across the dentils is heavier. The file marks from the lapping are quite visible. The cracks on the obverse are somewhat heavier, also.

Rarity 2

B25

OBVERSE 17—used on **B25** only. There is a "whisker" on the underside of the chin near the throat. There is a heavy lump in the field about a third of the distance between the neck and star 12. On later states, cracks develop, under the lowest curl, through the bottoms of 17, up through 98 to the bottom of the bust. This crack goes to the left through or near all the stars on the left, down through LIBERTY and all of the stars on the right, to the bust. Radial cracks appear up through the 1 in the date and from the rim touching the right side of star 7.

REVERSE T-3, 5, 4, 5—used on **B24** and **B25**. See description of **B24**.

Die State a: The obverse has no cracks, just the whisker and the heavy lump mentioned above. There is a small break at the bottom of the stem to the dentils below.

Die State b: Cracks circle the obverse, plus a vertical crack through 1 in the date. The crack at the stem is heavier.

Die State c: The cracks are heavy. A new radial crack connects the right side of star 7 to the dentils.

Die State d: The cracks are very heavy, with the field sinking outside of the circular crack. Another radial crack, just left of the B in LIBERTY.

Rarity 3

B26

OBVERSE 13—used on **B26**, **B27**, **B28**, **B29**, **B30**, **B31**, **B33**. The 8 in the date is very high and leans left. A bar goes down to the left near the hair under IB. A series of bars runs slightly down to the left from between stars 10 and 11 toward between the lower lip and the chin. A short, heavier bar from below the left point of star 12 toward the top of the neck. A triple crack from the dentils under the nine curves to the left up through star 1 into the field. A second branch runs up through the center of 9. A third branch curves up to the right through the dentils up toward the bottom of the bust.

REVERSE L-3, 5, 4, 6—used only on **B26**. Like the obverse, there is a triple crack (really a 4-way crack) from near the bottom of the stem. The heavy crack starts in the dentils, up through the tip of the stem, up slightly to the left to the shield under the fifth group of vertical bars, to form heavy lumps which fill the lower third of the fifth group. Another crack, to the left, runs from near the bottom of the tip of the stem, across the tail feathers, through the arrows, through E4, through the left wing, the first cloud, to the bottom of T2. There is a heavy short crack in the tail feathers below the previous crack. The fourth crack from the bottom of the stem goes up to the right, the bottom of A3, four of the leaves on the right, the right ribbon end, up to left through the right wing, cloud 8, bottom of O, tops of S2-E2-T3. There is a short parallel crack under the right claw to the bottom of A3.

There are some heavy short cracks up through the left top of T2. A very heavy double crack with a third lighter crack on the right, at the right top of T3. A heavy crack runs up from the left tip of E2, with another going up from cloud 5, just missing the left tip of S2, through the right tip of E2 to the dentils above. Another crack runs from the dentils near F, over the right wing tip, tops of AM to the dentils over E3.

Rarity 4

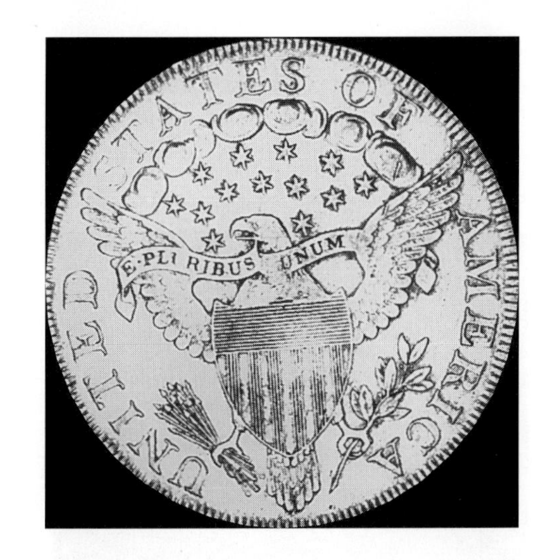

B27

OBVERSE 13—used on **B26**, **B27**, **B28**, **B29**, **B30**, **B31**, and **B33**. This die was used first, before the cracks in **B27**. Everything else is the same on the two dies. The item that matches **B27** with **B26** is the bar from below the left point of star 12 toward the top of the neck, seen on all of the coins struck with this die.

REVERSE K-1, 2, 3, 4—used on **B11**, **B15**, **B16**, and **B27**. The third berry from the top is tiny, and attached to a leaf point.

Die State a: Other than the bar at star 12, the coin has no defects.

Die State b: Another bar has been added to the one at star 12. Crack runs from over E2-S2-OF-right wing tip, rim over A2.

Rarity 2

B28

OBVERSE 13—used on **B26**, **B27**, **B28**, **B29**, **B30**, **B31**, **B33**. See description of **B26**. The only difference is that a second bar at star 12 was added for **B27**. Now a third has been added for **B28**.

REVERSE P-1, 5, 5, 6—used only on **B28**. The left upright of N1 has been tripled, with extra uprights on the right and left. Sometimes the left line disappears, but the one on the right has been seen on every **B28** inspected. There are thirteen perfect arrowheads and shafts, some of the best seen.

Die State a: Reverse perfect.

Die State b: The reverse is cracked from the rim up through the arrow feather ends.

Die State c: A heavy crack from the rim to the most left tail feathers to the left leg of the eagle. The section between cracks b and is now rising.

Die State d: Four sections of the coin between the two cracks at the tail have risen.

Die State e: The sections which have risen are growing larger.
Die State f: The entire section between the two cracks is now one smooth cud.

Rarity 3

B29

OBVERSE 13—used on **B26**, **B27**, **B28**, **B29**, **B30**, **B31**, and **B33**. See description of **B26**. The cracks are like **B26**, but heavier, with some additions. The crack from under the 9 to the right now crosses the bust, ending in a lump near star 13. There are now four lumps near star 12.

REVERSE Q-5, 5, 5, 6—used on **B12** and **B29**. **B29** might have been struck first. One example of **B29** has all thirteen stars showing on the reverse, with only the center one somewhat weak. The second example has ten stars showing. On **B12**, the example has seven stars showing, and is probably a later strike using the same die.
Die State a: On the reverse, all thirteen stars are present, but the center star is weak.
Die State b: On the reverse, seven strong stars show, plus three weak stars.

Rarity 4

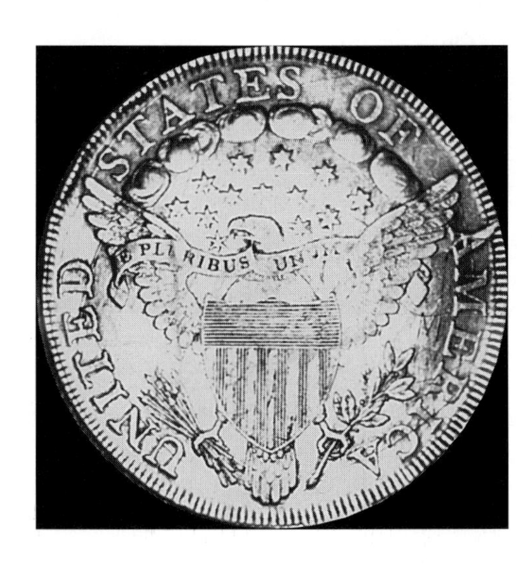

B30

OBVERSE 13—used on **B26**, **B27**, **B28**, **B29**, **B30**, **B31** and **B33**. See description of **B26**. "Stairs" up from I to B. Dull line over IBERTY, another under tops of TY, tops of stars 8 and 9.

REVERSE N-3, 3, 3, 5—used on **B30** only. Stars are all distant from clouds.
Die State a: Obverse and reverse perfect. Have not seen this variety, but it is believed to exist.

Die State b: Obverse has the standard cracks of **B26**. Reverse has many cracks.

1. From the end of the feathers closest to the dentils through UN, bottoms of ITE.
2. From the dentils over N, top of T1, center of E, bottom of D, four feathers, clouds 1, 2, and 3, bottoms of TE, up through S, dentils over O.
3. Top of D, two wing tips, S1, T2, over A1, dentils.
4. Up through O, top of F, curves down to meet crack 5.
5. From top of wing near cloud 8, over right side of cloud 8 to wing near tip, top two feathers, centers of AM, curves down through right foot of M through right wing to star 12.
6. From cloud 8 to right point of star 13.
7. Point up from scroll over M.
8. Curved crack connects stars 12 and 13.
9. Crack from wing near scroll touches crack 8.
10. Crack from star 9 to I on scroll.
11. Crack from cloud two to star 7 to left wing over U.
12. Crack from right top of M, E3, right serif of upright of R, leaves, curving up through shield, right top of vertical group 6, up to the left through all of the horizontal lines through U2, eagle's head.
13. Crack from top of R1, down through ICA, across stem, arrow feathers.
14. Heavy cud form from edge of coin over left side of A2 down to the left side of the right foot of A2, to a lump below A2, feather.

Rarity 4

B31

OBVERSE 13—used on **B26**, **B27**, **B28**, **B29**, **B30**, **B31**, and **B33**. See description of **B26**. The cracks seem weaker on this variety. Many spikes come through the tops of LIBERTY. Two connected longer spikes are between the B and the E. Below the tops, they are connected with a long spike.

REVERSE M-3, 5, 4, 6—used on **B31** only. The top three berries are very tiny. The two lower berries are normal. The upper three have no stems, but the lower two have stems. Of the six stars left of center, only the left three in the upper row are strong. On the second row, the left star is strong, and the center star, over the head of the eagle, is weak. The three left stars on the right are strong. On the right side, the upper two rows are gone, and the three on the lowest row are present. Eight of the stars are fairly strong, and one is weak. The other five are missing.

Die State a: The cracks on **B26** are present, but weak. The spikes above LIBERTY are sharp.

Die State b: The obverse is as it should be, with the cracks from **B26** fairly strong. The reverse, however, has many cracks.

1. The lines are fairly well filled at the bottom of the 5th group of lines in the shield.
2. A very heavy crack from the rim under the blob down through the point of the stem down to the dentils.
3. A heavy crack from the point of the stem crosses the tail feathers, through the arrows, through E4 in the scroll, across the left wing, cloud 1, the bottom of T2, up through T2 to the dentils.

4. Two very heavy lines connect the right side of dentils above.

5. A heavy line goes up from the left lower serif of E2 halfway up the E.

6. A heavy crack from a dentil over the right side of E2 touches the right top corner of E2, just misses the S to the cloud below.

7. A fine crack from the right top of E2, runs through the top of S2, bottom of O, cloud 8, across the right wing, through the tip of the scroll, through all four right leaves, bottom of A2, where it crosses the tail to the arrows.

Rarity 4

B32

OBVERSE 2—used on 1797 **B1**, 1798 **B1**, and **B32**. Obverse cracked from star 3, to star 4, to ribbon. Crack from bust down to dentils. Another crack from bust just right of 8 to dentils. Star 6 is weak and star 7 is practically gone because the die is sinking. There is a lump near the outside point of star 9.

REVERSE C-4, 4, 3, 5—used on **B4** and **B32**. The third arrowhead from the left has a very weak arrowhead and shaft. The third from the right has no arrowhead. There are lines up to the left between A1 and T3.

Die State a: Die is good. All of the stars are strong.

Die State b: Die is sinking. Stars 5, 6, and 7 disappear, as does the L.

Rarity 6

B33
OBVERSE 13—used on **B26**, **B27**, **B28**, **B29**, **B30**, **B31**, and **B33**. See description of **B26**.

REVERSE O-3, 5, 4, 6—used only on **B33**. Thirteen nice arrows. A very heavy crack from the dentils through the right side of T1. A lighter crack runs from the dentils over the M, through both left serifs of M to the curl in the scroll below. A large raised elongated lump, running across the eagle's throat just below the scroll, connects these two cracks.

Rarity 8

Chapter Six:

Rapid Finder For 1799

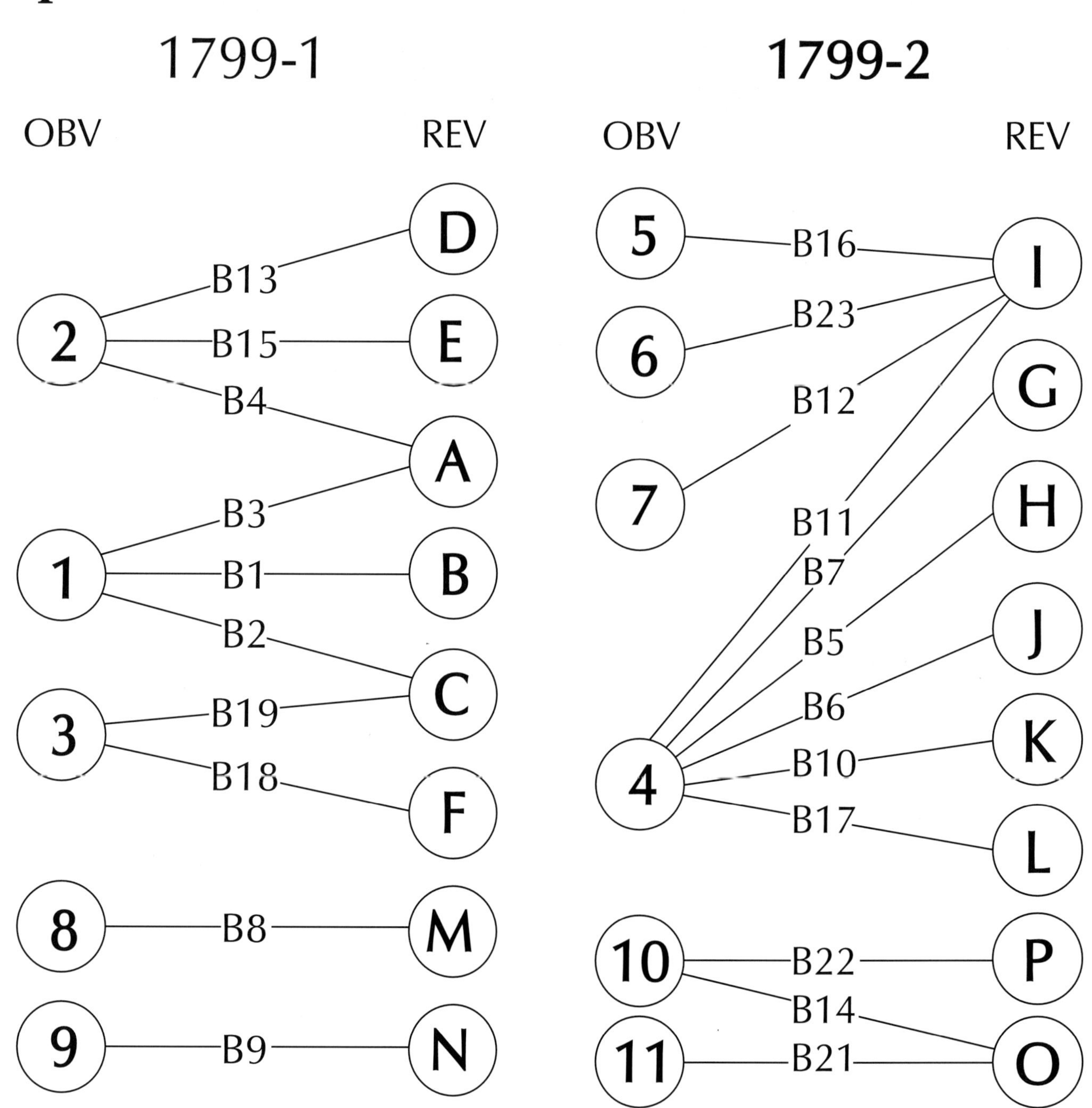

SEE APPENDIX A FOR LOCATION NUMBERS

Appendix No.	Bolender No.	Description
3545	B15	**REVERSE** E—heavy lumps connect tip of stem to rim.
	B15	**OBVERSE** 2—used on B4, B13, and B15. Star 8 has 1 point. doubled, and star 9 has two. Star 13 touches the drapery.
3546	B13	**REVERSE** D—lumps in and over E2.
	B15	See obverse 2 above.
3546	B7	**REVERSE** G—many cracks on reverse. Very heavy vertical crack through left side of S2.
	B7	**OBVERSE** 4—used on B5, B6, B7, B10, B11, B17; star 13 distant 2mm from bust.
4535	B3, B4	**REVERSE** A—the well-known fifteen star reverse. Fifteen stars were punched into the reverse die. When it was discovered, the two on the ends of the upper row were partially covered by lowering the end clouds. Points of both stars protrude through the clouds, however.
	B3	**OBVERSE**—9 is punched over an 8. Star 13 is distant from bust.
	B4	**OBVERSE**—cracks run around the entire obverse. Star 13 touches drapery on bust.
543(5)	B11, B12, B16, B23	**REVERSE** I—The berries slowly disappear. #1 B16—all five berries are present, with the second berry from the top rather weak. #2 B23—The two upper berries are almost gone, and the three lower berries are weak. #3 B12—All five berries are gone, with the stem from the second berry from the bottom still present. #4 B11—Everything is gone, with a tiny bit of the stem on B12 still visible.
5435	B10	**REVERSE** K—a beautiful reverse. The only defect is a tiny horizontal crack from the bottom of the claw around the stem horizontal to the tail feathers.
	B10	**OBVERSE** 4—also used on B5, B6, B7, B11, and B17.
5435	B17	**REVERSE** L—five large berries, the upper two buried in leaves. There are many small lumps around the arrow feathers. A dull spike from the bottom of the stem runs down to the left.
	B17	**OBVERSE** 4—also used on B5, B6, B7, B10, and B11.
5535	B18	**REVERSE** F—a sharp spike from the bottom of the stem runs down to the right.
	B18	**OBVERSE** 3—also used on B19.
5545	B5	**REVERSE** H—the left side of the left serif of U is missing.
	B5	**OBVERSE** 4—used on B5, B6, B7, B10, B11, and B17.
5546	B1	**REVERSE** B—A heavy lump connects right top of T2 to dentils above. A very heavy blob covers the left side and top of I2.
	B1	**OBVERSE**—used on B1, B2, and B3.
5546	B8	**REVERSE** M—heavy lumps at the top of S2. Clash marks of the bust are farther left than usual.
	B8	**OBVERSE** 8.
5546	B14 and B21.	**REVERSE** O—heavy lumps in the shield between most of the vertical lines.
	B14	**OBVERSE** 10—used on B14 and B22.
	B21	**OBVERSE** 11.
5546	B22	**REVERSE** P—a heavy horizontal crack runs across the reverse from E1 below the banner, to M. The left serif of U is gone.
	B22	**OBVERSE** 10—used on B14 and B22.
5557	B6	**REVERSE** J—a curved crack, left of O from the rim to cloud 7.
	B6	**OBVERSE** 4—used on B5, B6, B7, B10, B11, and B17.
5557	B9	**REVERSE** N—a heavy lump from the dentils right of S2.
	B9	**OBVERSE** 9.

6535	B2, B19	**REVERSE** C—a heavy crack up to the right from the right side of D to the dentils.
	B2	**OBVERSE** 1—second 9 in date is over an 8.
	B19	**OBVERSE** 3—crack from rim, star 3, star 2; star 1, date

B1

OBVERSE 1—used on **B1**, **B2**, and **B3**. Date 9/8. Both the obverse and reverse dies contained many pits, with the coins having corresponding lumps. On obverse 1 we have the following:

1. Small lumps between 7 and 9 in the date, others in the first 9.
2. A low spot in the drapery over the second 9 contains a long lump.
3. Lumps between star 7 and bottom of L.
4. Heavy long lump down to right at left bottom of E.
5. Heavy long line above upright of R.
6. Series of lumps and lines under center of R to left upright of T.
7. Group of lumps behind head above ribbon.
8. There are small lumps inside the curls.

REVERSE B-5, 5, 4, 6—used only on **B1**.

1. A heavy group of lumps at the right top of T2 connects the right top to the dentils above.
2. There are many lumps between T2 and A1.
3. A very heavy group of lumps connects the top of I2 to the dentils, down through the foot of R, with lumps over the left side of C, and others to the leaves below and between I and C.
4. There are lumps between stars 1 and 2 and 1 and 7. There is a vertical line between stars 8 and 9.
5. A light crack from below the center of S2 to the top of O to a dentil
6. A lighter crack from the same point on S2 goes to the lower part of OF. Lumps appear between cracks 5 and 6.

Die State a: As described above.

Die State b: Additional lumps between 1 and star 1 on the obverse.

Reverse crack 5 is now heavy. It continues to the left through S2, bottom of E, clouds on left, with more lumps.

Reverse crack 6 is very heavy, with additional lumps, through the right wing.

Rarity 3

B2

OBVERSE 1—used on **B1**, **B2**, and **B3**. Date 1799/8. See description of **B1**. All of the items listed for **B1** are present except for item #5. This die probably was used first on **B2**, then on **B1**. Several of the other lumps were slightly smaller on **B2** than on **B1**.

REVERSE C-6, 5, 3, 5—used on **B2** and **B19**. Many lumps appear on this die:
1. A lump appears between the bottom of N1 and the second arrowhead from the left.
2. There are lumps and lines under E1.
3. A heavy line from the right side of D, above the center, goes up to the right to a dentil.
4. A small lump is near the dentils over the left foot of A2.
5. Many small lumps run from near the tips of the feathers under the left side of E3—up to the right between E and R—almost to the dentils.

Rarity 4

B3

OBVERSE 1—used on **B1**, **B2**, and **B3**. Date 1799/8. See description of **B1**. All of the items on **B1** are present, several of them heavier. Item #4, the long lump at the left bottom of E is now doubled. As was stated in **B2**, it is likely that this die was used first on **B2**, then on **B1**, and third on **B3**.

REVERSE A-4, 5, 3, 5—used on **B3** and **B4**. This is the well-known fifteen star reverse. The engraver put in seven stars on the top row, six in the second row, and two on the bottom row, for a total of fifteen stars. He tried to cover the mistake by pulling down the two end clouds on the top row. Two points of star 1 have about half of each showing. On the 7th star, the cloud comes down a bit more, and the left tip shows, but only a tiny bit of the right tip. The clouds are so deep that the error would have been known to all. There are a few dots right of D, a crack near the dentils over ATES, and a heavy clash mark over OF.

Rarity 3

B4

OBVERSE 2—used on **B4**, **B13**, and **B15**. From studying the cracks, it seems that this die was used first on **B13**, then **B15**, and finally on **B4**. On **B4** there is a heavy lump between the two left points of star 4. This lump is not seen on **B13** and **B15**. A point of star 13 touches the top of the drapery just before the drapery touches the bust. This is seen on all three varieties. Stars 1, 2, and 3 are very close to each other, but the other stars on the left are fairly distant from each other. On the right, star 8 is fairly close to star 9. There are many cracks on the obverse, listed under die states.

REVERSE A-4, 5, 3, 5—used on **B3** and **B4**. The fifteen star reverse. See description of **B3**. Other than the fifteen stars and the heavy clouds, the dots, crack, and clash mark are not present. This seems to indicate that the die was used first on **B4**, then on **B3**.

Die States a:

OBVERSE

1-Crack goes from the dentils between stars 4 and 5, through stars 4, 3, 2, 1 just above the bottoms of the date, to the dentils a little over halfway between the date and the tip of the bust.

2-Crack from the end of crack 1 up through the drapery.

3-Crack from star 1 to the second curl from the bottom, up through the drapery over the date, curves up across the bust near stars 13, 12, and 11 up through stars 10, 9, center of star 8, up through Y, to the dentils over T.

4-Crack from the centers of stars 4, 5, and 6, upper left of star 7, dentils over left side of L.

5-Crack from the center of star 7 runs through LIB, top of E, rim between E and R.

6,7,8-Three cracks from the rim to the top of R; 6 from the rim to over the left top of R; 7 on to the right side of the upright of R, down through the R almost to the toe; 8 and the third, heavier, down through the right side of R to the bottom of T, under the Y to the tip of the nose across the upper lip to the neck.

9-Fine crack from #3 - to the upper left point of star 10.

10-Light crack from star 10 up to the left to the dentils.

11-Second crack from star 10 down to the right to dentils at star 11.

REVERSE a: The well-known fifteen star reverse. No defects are to be found on state a.

OBVERSE b: Has all of the cracks of state a, heavier, plus

12-Heavy vertical crack from #1, just right of the second 9, across the drapery to crack 3.

13-Cracks 9, 10, and 11 are all very heavy.

14-An extremely heavy crack from crack 3, upper left point of star 12, just misses the upper right tip of star 12, to the center of a crack covering three dentils.

REVERSE b:

15-The dots right of D are present, as is the crack over ATES, but it is very light. The fact that the clash mark over OF is not present, bears out the theory that reverse A was first on **B4**, then on **B3**.

Rarity 3

B5

OBVERSE 4, used on **B5**, **B6**, **B7**, **B10**, **B11**, and **B17**. Star 1 is slightly small and thin. There is a strong dot in the heavy fold in the drapery over the center of the first 9 in the date, and tiny dots just inside the lowest fold in the drapery just right of the 1 and between the 9s in the date. Star 13 is very distant from the bust.

REVERSE H-5, 5, 4, 5—used only on **B5**. The left side of the left serif of U is missing. This is also true of **B16**, so the same U punch must have been used for both. The dies are not the same, however. On **B5** the third star from the left points to the right side of the base of T, while on **B16** it points between T and E. On **B5** the right star in the top row has two points touching the cloud above, while on **B16** only one point touches.

Die State a: No cracks on either obverse or reverse. (I have not seen this variety, but it is reported by Bolender.)

Die State b:

OBVERSE 1—Crack through the point of the left dentil of E down through the hair meets a crack from the dentils below star 1.

REVERSE 2—Crack on the reverse runs from the center of U—up through N I to top of TED through the feathers, to the centers of STA, to the tops of TES.

Rarity 4

B6

OBVERSE 4—used on **B5**, **B6**, **B7**, **B10**, **B11**, and **B17**. See description of **B5**. Star 1 is now even smaller.

REVERSE J-5, 5, 5, 7—used only on **B6**. Serifs of U are perfect. T2 touches cloud 2 and A1 touches cloud 3.

Die State a:

1-Heavy crack curves down to the right, from the dentils. All on reverse, to cloud 7.

2-Faint crack from below the top of O down to the right through the center of F to the upper wing tip.

3-Lumps and lines between the tops of A and M.

4-Light crack from the right serif of the left foot of R - to the leaves under IC.

Die State b:

5-Short crack curved up from the top serif of E1.

6-Crack from cloud 1-under S1-through bottom of T2-to the center of A1.

7-Crack from the dentils just right of S2, to the cloud below.

8-Crack from the dentils over wing tip 3, the top of A2, lumps and lines in 3—down through M—bottoms of ER, to the leaf under I, to the inner leaf under C.

Rarity 3

B7

OBVERSE 4—Used on **B5**, **B6**, **B7**, **B10**, **B11**, and **B17**. See description of **B5**.

REVERSE G—3, 5, 4, 6, used only on **B7**. Of the six stars in the top row, the two on the left and the two on the right each have two points touching the clouds, and the center two each have only one point touching.

Die States:

Bolender lists this variety without breaks and with. I have not seen it without breaks, but it would be state a if it exists. This one is:

7b OBVERSE

1-Crack from dentils below star 1 toward curls.

2-A twisting crack from the top of B goes down to the I below the top.

3-There is a crack down to the left in the upper part of B.

4-The top of the 1 is perfect. Either this variety was made before the punch broke, or the die has been repaired.

5-The diagonal line at the throat is visible.

REVERSE

6-Crack runs from the bottoms of E3, RICA, the stem, about 1/8" above the bottom, all of the tail feathers, the two lowest arrow feathers, the bottoms of UNITED, to the upper left wing tip.

7-Heavy crack from the dentils left of U to crack 6.

8-Faint crack from the tip of the top left feather to the tops of ST2.

9-Crack through the centers of STA.

10-Crack from the dentils over the left top of M, through the bottom of the right upright, curves through the second tail feather on the right, up through the left upper point of the shield, across the banner between L and U, clouds 1 and 2, the left foot of A1, the top of T3 to the dentils.

11-There is a small raised section between the tops of T and E.

12-Crack goes through the bases of ATES.

13-Very heavy crack comes down from the dentils through the left side of S2.

14-Crack from the dentils left of O through the top of F, to the top right wing tip.

15-Crack runs from near the bottom of F across three tail feathers to the bottom of A2. The section of the die holding the three tips breaks away from the die, and that section rises like a cud.

Rarity 4

B8

OBVERSE 8—used only on **B8**. In the date, the 1 and 7 lean to the right, and the two 9s lean left, the second one more than the first 9. The left point of star 10 is heavily doubled. The high wave of the hair is centered under the right side of E, and the wave of the hair to the right is under the foot of R. On the obverse of **B12**, which is similar to **B8**, the wave under the R is to the left, almost under the center of R.

REVERSE M-5, 5, 4, 6—used only on **B8**. Many lumps inside and right of the top of S2. An extra serif (where no serif is used) is at the right bottom of N. It is probably from an upside down N, or from an I. I have not seen this die state, but have seen states b and c.

Die State a: As above.

Die State b:

OBVERSE

1-Crack from the rim at star 6, through the two upper points of star 7, upright of L, tip of right serif of L, up through I, center of B. A short crack from the top of star 7-down to the right, crosses this crack.

REVERSE

2-There is a series of lumps over D and to the right, at the end of the wing tips.

3-There is a faint crack over STA-to the rim over T.

4-Faint crack runs through clouds 1, 2, and 3-the bottom of T, the center of E, the top of S.

5-Heavy crack from the dentil to the center of S2, then thin to the center of S2.

6-Crack 4 continues from the right top of S2, very heavy for a short distance, then lighter to the center of O, down through O to the left foot of F.

7-Two very heavy, but dull, cracks go from the center of crack 6, forming a heavy arc up to the dentils and down to the top of O, with a second one, below, going through the top of O to the center of the right side of O.

8-Very fine crack from the right top serif of F, curves through the arrows.

9-Three parallel cracks run from the bottom of E, at the right side of the upright run down into the field.

10-Crack from the right side of A3 crosses the stem about 1/8" from the end, the tail feathers, the arrow feathers, to the right top of U.

Rarity 3

B9

OBVERSE 9—used only on **B9**. The obverse die is very ordinary. The coin is easily identified by the heavy break at the right of S2 on the reverse, which causes the coin to be known as the "Apostrophe S" because of the heavy lump at the dentils after S2. Many of the obverses have a heavy line up from the dentils under the 1 in the date. Some have a series of lumps down to the left from the bottom of I. Some of the later die states have cracks in the lower curls. Early states may have none of these defects, but they all have the "Apostrophe" at S2.

REVERSE N-5, 5, 5, 7—used only on **B9**. As stated in obverse, this is called the "Apostrophe S". There are many reverse cracks, but these vary with the die state.

Die States **Note:** I have seen four of this variety, each one with a different die state. There may be additional states, but this is true of every variety.

Die State a:

OBVERSE, no visible cracks.

REVERSE

1-Apostrophe is single, fairly heavy.

2-Very light crack from the dentils over left side of M, down through the top of E, down through RIC.

3-Very faint crack top of ICA.

4-Crack from the dentils to the second and third left wing tips.

5-There is a crack above the upper left wing tip.

Dic State b:

OBVERSE

6-Series of small lumps runs from the dentils between I and B, down to the left under I.

7-Crack from the dentils, through the center of the 10th star, chin, neck above throat, drapery, right side of first 9.

REVERSE

8-Apostrophe is heavier at the top.

9-Crack 2 is rather strong.

10-Crack 5 splits into two cracks.

Die State c:

OBVERSE

11-A heavy crack from the dentils, halfway to the bottom of 1.

REVERSE

12-The apostrophe now has another crack touching the original one on the left side from the top to the center.

13-Crack 4 now has two parallel lines, one touching the second feather on the left, and one touching the third feather, both from the top.

Die State d:

OBVERSE

14-Crack 11 now is longer, touching the bottom of 1.

15-Crack from the dentils right of the second 9 up to the right to the dentils.

REVERSE

16-The apostrophe is now 3 cracks wide, almost touching the S.

17-Very heavy line from a dentil over the left side of S2 almost touches that letter. Many lines and dots around S. Many lines up from the tops of most of the letters.

18-There is a fine clash mark through OF.

19-Crack from the dentils down to the right to the left top of M, down through ERICA.

Rarity 2

B10

OBVERSE 4—used on **B5**, **B6**, **B7**, **B10**, **B11**, and **B17**. See description **B5**. A fine crack connects stars 11, 12, and 13.

REVERSE K-5, 4, 3, 5—used only on **B10**. Stars 1, 3, 4, and 6 each have one point touching a cloud. Stars 2 and 5 each have two points touching clouds.

Die State a:

OBVERSE

1-A faint crack runs through stars 10, 11, 12, 13.

REVERSE

2-There is a heavy crack across the four feathers of the right wing, touching the fifth feather through RI.

Die State b:

3-Crack from the dentils over S2 goes through the centers of OF, three right wing tips, bottoms of AME, up through RI.

4-Very heavy crack from the dentils down through the right side of O, curves around to the center of the bottom of O.

5-Heavy crack from the junction of 3 and 4 to the left for a short distance, then down through the bottom of O, forming a cross in the O.

6-Crack from the bottoms of ICA, through the bottom of the eagle's right foot, through a lump in the right side of the eagle's tail feathers, through the eagle's left claw, up through the arrows, across the four feathers of the left wing, up through ST to the tip of A1, to the dentils almost over T3.

7-Crack from the wing near crack 3, across the wing, across the right end of the banner, into the field

8-Crack through the field and stem, missing all the berries.

Rarity 3

B11

OBVERSE 4—used on **B5**, **B6**, **B7**, **B10**, **B11**, and **B17**. See description **B5**. This die is a real enigma. From the positions of the letters, stars, etc., it seems to be from the same die. There are several differences, however. Here are the differences:

1. On most of the coins listed for this obverse, the first star is small and weak. On **B11** it is slightly smaller than the other stars in **B10**, but strong.

2. On all of the others there is a heavy dot in the second fold in the drapery. The dot is not on **B11**.

3. On the others star 13 is 1/8" from the drapery on the bust. On **B11** it is not quite that far away.

4. **B11** has a heavy dot between star 13 and the L, just under the bottom of L. I cannot find this on any of the others.

For the reasons mentioned above, I feel that this is a different obverse.

Here are the characteristics:

The stars are all strong, including star 1. Star 1 is slightly smaller than the others. The top of the 1 is perfect, but it looks like it has been built up. There is a diagonal line under the throat, as on some of the other varieties using obverse 4, but it is different on **B11**. Early states of **B11** have a straight line with a curve at the top. On other dies using **B4** the line is straight. On later states of **B11**, additional lines are added. On all of the **B11**s, there are many heavy clash marks, with several sets of waves over the date, among other clash marks.

REVERSE I-5, 4, 3, (5)—used on **B11**, **B12**, **B16**, and B23. The left serif of U is missing. The die was first used on **B16**. All five berries and stems are strong. The die was then used on B23. The three lower berries are strong, the two upper ones very weak on the late die states. The third use was on **B12**, where only the third berry is still seen, but it is very weak. On the final use, **B11**, all of the berries are gone, and only one or two stems remain.

Die State a:

1-Heavy crack develops from the rim to the center of the right side of D, to the fourth feather from the top of the left wing, to the upper left tip of star 12, to the top center point of star 12.

2-A branch of this crack goes down through the right side of to the left tip of the scroll.

3-Clash marks through OF.

Die State b:

4-Crack 1 is now heavier and longer. It goes from the center of the right side of D - down through the right side of D, through the tip of the scroll, past the feathers (touching one of them) down through the left side of the shield.

5-Crack from the top of star 12, through the right side of star 7, through cloud 2.

Rarity 3

B12

OBVERSE 7—used only on **B12**. Star 1 is quite distant from the lowest two curls, almost at the level of the third curl. This variety is best identified by the cracks on the obverse, and by the berries (or lack of them) on the reverse.

REVERSE I-5, 4, 3, (5)—used on **B11**, **B12**, **B16**, and **B23**. See reverse of **B11**.

Die State a:

1-obverse perfect.

Die State b:

2-There is a crack from the dentils under the right side of 7, bottom of 1, into the field near star 1.

3-Crack from the dentils under the first 9 up to the bottom of that 9.

4-Crack from just under the bottom of the serif of the 7 down through the bottom of the first 9, then up to the right to near the tip of the second 9.

5-Crack from the dentils right of the second 9 curves up to under the bust.

Die State c:

6-Crack 3 runs through the bottom of the first 9, and goes up slightly to the left to join the loop of the first 9 near the left side.

7-Crack 5 curves up to the left across the bust, bottom of the neck, bottom of the ear, across the hair, down to star 2.

8-Weaker crack comes out of crack 5 to near the tip of the bust.

9-Crack from the dentils near the top of the bust curves up through the center of the field to two points of star 9.

10-Short crack from star 13 runs down to the right to the dentils.

11-Crack from star 10 curves from the upper point to the dentils at star 11.

12-Crack from the rim to the upper point of star 1.

13-Crack runs from star 1 to star 2, and from star 2 to star 3.

Rarity 3

B13
OBVERSE 2—used on **B4**, **B13**, and **B15**. See description of **B4**.

REVERSE D-3, 5, 4, 6—used on **B13**. There is a lump over the top of E2, another touching the point of the right top serif and a third inside of the upper half of E2. There are lumps around the two lowest stars on the right. There are almost horizontal lines between vertical stripes 4 to 5, and 5 to 6.

Rarity 5

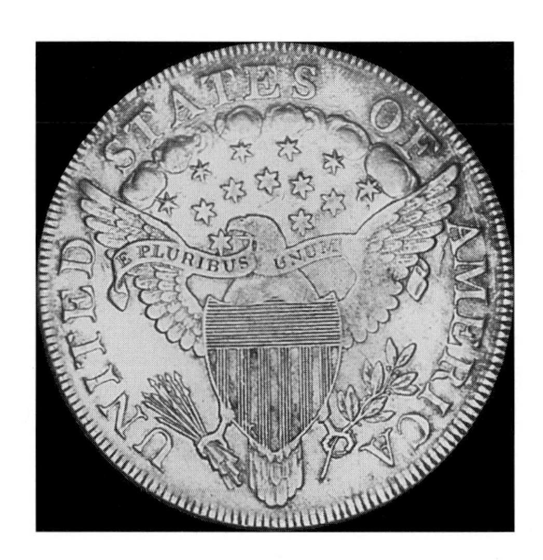

B14
OBVERSE 10—used on **B14** and **B22**. One heavy lump and one small round dot about one third of the distance between the eyeball and star 9. The right point of star 10 points to a lump at the base of a dentil. There are some tiny lumps between the bottoms of Y and star 8.

REVERSE O-5, 5, 4, 6—used on **B14** and **B21**. Heavy lumps under AM. Lumps at star on far right, and next to star behind eagle's head. Heavy lumps in shield between most of the stripes.

Rarity 3

B15

OBVERSE 2—used on **B4**, **B13**, and **B15**. See description of **B4**.

REVERSE E-3, 5, 4, 5—used on 1798 **B24**, 1798 **B25**, and 1799 **B15**. Two die breaks connect the stem to the border below.

Die State a:

1-Light crack through outer points of stars 1- 4.

2-In addition to the heavy breaks mentioned above, there are two heavy lumps from the dentils about a third of the way from the lumps mentioned above to A3.

Die State b:

3-Second crack goes from the inside of star 4, through the centers of stars 5 and 6, to the outer tip of star 7.

4-Third crack runs from the inside of star 7, up through LIBE-to the rim between E and R.

5-Crack runs from the rim to the top of R.

6-Heavy crack runs from the center of the top of R, down through the bottom of T, underneath the Y, where it curves to the tip of the nose.

7-Very heavy crack from the rim goes to the left top of Y, through the center of star 8, down through the bottom of star 9, the lower tip of star 10, under the other stars to the bust.

8-Straight horizontal crack runs through the date just above the bottoms, to the rim at the right.

9-Crack from the second curl from the bottom to star 1.

10-Crack runs from near the date to star 1.

Rarity 5

B16

OBVERSE 5—used only on **B16**. Stars 1 and 7, on the left side, are both distant from the curl and the L, approximately 3mm. Stars 8 and 13, on the right side, are roughly 1mm from the Y and the bust.

REVERSE I-5, 4, 3, (5)—used on **B11**, **B12**, **B16** and **B23**. See description of reverse 11.

Die State a:

1-Perfect, no defects.

Die State b:

2-Clash marks look like waves over date.

3-Heavy crack from the rim right of the date, curves up to the left, toward another crack.

4-Crack from the junction of crack 3 and the bust goes down to the right to the dentils.

5-Crack from crack 3 runs vertically up 1mm from the neck, to the throat.

6-Crack from near the neck curves up below the lowest curl on the neck, then down toward the second curl from the top.

7-Short heavy crack runs down from the upright of E.

8-Some tiny cracks from the right side of R.

9-Short vertical crack from the right tip of the left serif of R, to the top of hair curl under R.

10-Heavy crack from the rim to star 9, curves through the inner point of star 9 to the center of the nose.

11-Crack from star 10 curves right of star 11 to the rim at star 12.

12-Heavy clash marks around star 12 and below bust.

13-Some heavy clash marks at the bust near the throat.

14-Sharp crack runs from the rim through the upper points of star 1 into the field.

15-Crack runs from the outer points of star 3 to star 6.

Die State c:

16-There are several clash marks, plus a heavy crack, left of the date.

17-Cracks and clash marks in state b are heavy, plus heavy cracks and clash marks from the rim through the lowest curl, close under the bust over 179.

18-Many additional clash marks, plus some cracks, around stars 12 and 13.

Rarity 3

B17

OBVERSE 4—used on **B5**, **B6**, **B7**, **B10**, **B11**, and **B17**. See description of **B5**. There is a heavy crack from the rim near star 9, through stars 10, 11, 12, and 13. There are very faint cracks at the foot of the dentils from star 3 to star 6.

REVERSE L-5, 4, 3, 5—used only on **B17**. Berries are extra large. The upper two are partially buried in the leaves. Below star 2 there are two very heavy almost horizontal lines, with heavy vertical lines at both ends.

Die State a: No cracks.

Die State b: On the reverse, there is a heavy crack from the dentils, down through the center of U, the bottoms of NITED, through the top three feathers, the center of S1, and the top of T2.

Rarity 3

B18

OBVERSE 3—used on **B18** and **B19**. The high wave of the hair is under the right edge of E, the farthest right of any other 1799 obverse. Stars 1 and 2 are doubled.

REVERSE F-5, 5, 3, 5—used only on **B18**. The left tip of the left serif of U is doubled. There is a heavy sharp point and several tiny points from the 2nd feather from the top on the right side, and a few tiny points from the 3rd.

Die State a: Perfect. There are no other cracks or flaws.

Die State b: 1-There is a fine crack from the dentils over R, down through ICA, stem, tail feathers, arrow feathers, under the U.

Die State c: 2-There is an extremely heavy crack from a very large dentil between E1 and D, to the bottom right of E1, across the left tip of the banner, the top of the third feather below the banner, to the left tip of the shield. There is a short crack up to the right in the space under RI in PLURIBUS.

Rarity 4

B19

OBVERSE 3—used on **B18** and **B19**. Stars 1, 2, and 3 are doubled. A very heavy crack from the dentil to the left center tip of star 3 to the left lower point of star 3. Another crack, not as heavy, runs from the left center tip of star 3 to the left upper tip of star 2, to the bottom tip of star 2, to the center of star 1, out the right center tip of star 1 just a trifle under the lowest curl, down through all four digits of the date, to the rim under the bust. This crack starts very heavy, and gets thinner as it goes, ending up very thin. Horizontal branches of this crack go from star 3 to a curl and from star 2 to a curl. A heavy vertical crack from the dentils goes straight down from the rim to the left of Y.

REVERSE C-6, 5, 3, 5—used on **B2** and **B19**. See description of the reverse of **B2**.

Rarity 5

Note: There is no **B20**. Haseltine's 20 was only a perfect example of **B18**. Bolender omitted this number in order to keep his numbers the same as Haseltine's. I see no reason to change this reasoning.

B21

OBVERSE 11—used only on **B21**. The lowest three points of star 2 are doubled. Star 1 is far (3mm) from the lowest curl. Star 7 is almost 2mm from L, and star 8 is close (1mm) to Y. The earliest die state seen has a faint crack from the dentils between 1 and 7, through the bottom of the first 9 to the center of the second 9. Both 9s have spikes from the center.

REVERSE O-5, 5, 4, 6—The earliest die state has heavy dashes down to the right under the center of A2,with a small dash under the center of M. There are heavy lumps in the left side of the shield, with very heavy lumps in the second series of lines and the space between the second and third series.

Die State a:

OBVERSE
One faint crack (1) up through both 9s.

REVERSE
No cracks, but lumps over E2, under AM.
Die State b:
OBVERSE
Crack (1), now extends to the bottom of the bust.

Rarity 3

B22

OBVERSE 10, used on **B14** and **B22**. There is a heavy bar, down slightly to the right, about 1/3 the distance between the eye and star 9.

REVERSE P-5, 5, 4, 6—used only on **B22**. This is an easy reverse to attribute, with a horizontal crack across the entire coin, just about the center of the coin. The lower half of the reverse seems to have risen slightly, with the upper half in the normal position. The crack runs from the rim to the right side of E1, with a large lump above the E and another below, across the tip of the pennant, the third feather below the pennant, across the eagle's breast between the bottom of the pennant and the top of the shield, between the sixth and seventh feathers of the right wing, up through the left side of M, to the dentils.

Die State a: The first lump from the left dentils is slightly connected to the top right serif of E1 by a short crack.

Die State b: The first lump from the left dentils is firmly mated to the top right serif of E1.

Rarity 5

B23

OBVERSE 6—used only on **B23**. This is a very easy variety to attribute, with eight stars on the left, and only five on the right. This is the only early dollar with such an arrangement.

REVERSE I-5, 4, 3, (5)—used on **B11**, **B12**, **B16**, and **B23**. The berries on this die become weaker and disappear. On the early state of this variety, the two lower berries are medium, and the third from the bottom is very weak, and the top two berries are gone.

Die State a: There is one obverse crack up to the right, through the right bottom of B, the left top of E, to the rim.

Die State b: Two small cracks form a V from the right top of B to the rim. The section formed by the V is raised, and looks like the start of a cud. Another curved crack from the rim, to star 3 to star 4, curves through star 7, to the rim. There are clash marks over the date, and on the reverse through OF.

Die State c: Heavy cracks around and over bust.

Rarity 4

Chapter Seven:

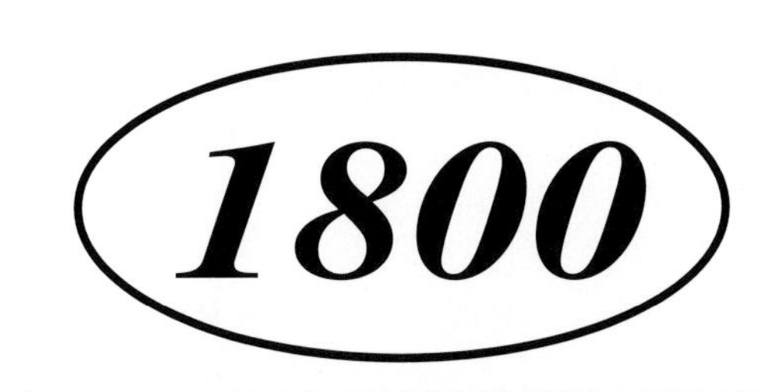

Rapid Finder For 1800

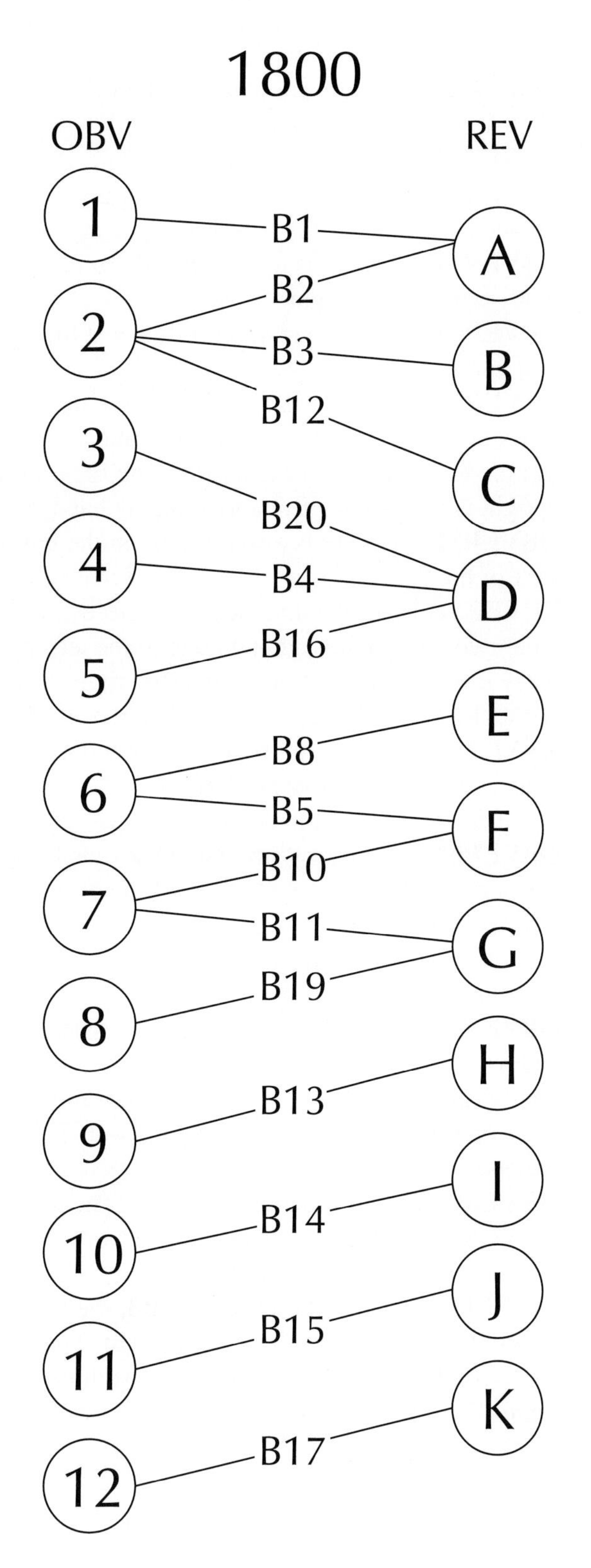

SEE APPENDIX A FOR LOCATION NUMBERS

Appendix No.	Bolender No.	Description
3546	B17	**REVERSE** K—dies were heavily clashed. The reverse has a very heavy clash mark through cloud 6 and OF.
	B17	**OBVERSE** 12—die clashing left a heavy clash mark on the bottom of the neck and the upper part of the bust, a "collar." There is a very heavy crack from the left side of 1 above the left serif, down to the left. The dies were lapped, removing the clash mark through OF, removing the "collar," and making the crack from the 1 very weak.
4435	B12	**REVERSE** C—there are lumps in the lower half of E1. There is a very heavy lump above the lower left serif of E3.
	B12	**OBVERSE** 2—used on B2, B3, and B12. R is heavily doubled.
4545	B5, B10	**REVERSE** F—there are tiny lumps in the upper half of S1, inside of A1, and between A1 and T3. There is a heavy lump on the tip of the banner under E1.
	B5	**OBVERSE** 6—there is a small but sharp lump in the bottom of R, above the right serif of the upright.
	B10	**OBVERSE** 7—there are several lumps at the tip of the bust, and between the bust and star 13.
4556	B8	**REVERSE** E—the serif at the top of the upright of F is different from any seen. It is a perfectly straight line, without the curve usually seen between the upright and the horizontal top of the letter. The first 1/2mm from the right side of the upright is very weak, probably done by hand. See B13 reverse.
	B8	**OBVERSE** 6—there is a sharp lump in the bottom of R, over the bottom right serif of the R.
4556	B15	**REVERSE** J—of the three top arrowheads, only the center one has a shaft. The other two, one to the right and one to the left, have no shafts at all. There are many tiny lumps, most of them to the right of S2.
	B15	**OBVERSE** 11—there is a tiny lump between R and T.
4557	B4, B16, B20	**REVERSE** D—bottom of T1 is sharply doubled. Upper right serif of T1 is long. A heavy lump touches left top of S2. A string of lumps runs from the right top of S2, up toward the dentils left of O.
	B4	**OBVERSE** 4—a heavy straight crack runs from the left bottom of 1 up slightly to the right to the bottom of the bust line near the hair.
	B16	**OBVERSE** 5—there is a strong dot even with the top of the hair, under the left side of E. A faint crack from the second O in the date curves up to the right, touching the chin, to star 10.
	B20	**OBVERSE** 3—some elongated dentils reach out to star 4, and between stars 5 and 6.
5546	B11 and B19	**REVERSE** G—a heavy crack runs from the junction of the stem and the left claw, curving right, to the rim right of A3. This is known as the Americai variety.
	B11	**OBVERSE** 7—used on B10 and B11. The hair curl under E is not complete.
	B19	**OBVERSE** 8—there are clash marks from the tail feathers on the reverse left of E to the rim to the left of R.
5546	B13	**REVERSE** H—like the reverse of B8, the line at the top of F has no curve where it joins the left side of the upright. The line is different from B8, because it is a solid line, while the line on B8 is quite weak for a short section from the right side of the upright.

5546	B14	**REVERSE** I—heavy lumps on right side of cloud 2, and between clouds 7 and 8.
	B14	**OBVERSE** 10—heavy lumps under, in, and over first O in date.
5556	B3	**REVERSE** B—there is a small dot on the center of the bottom of I2. Tip of the leaf under I2, the I in LIBERTY, touches the dot. An elongated lump lies between the right bottom of M and the tip of the banner.
	B3	**OBVERSE** 2—R in LIBERTY is doubled.
5657	B1 and B2	**REVERSE** A—T2, the first T in STATES, is sharply doubled. There are lumps left of the right claw.
	B1	**OBVERSE** 1—there are lumps inside of star 1, and all around star 11. Clash marks of 8 show between E and S.
	B2	**OBVERSE** 2—R in LIBERTY is doubled. A heavy lump connects the left side of B to the dentils above.

B1

OBVERSE 1—used only on **B1**. One almost touches lowest curl. There are several lumps on the obverse. A very heavy lump from the lowest right point of star 1 covers two thirds of the distance between star 1 and the third curl from the bottom. There is a smaller lump just above the lower left point of star 1. There is a lump between stars 1 and 2 to the right, and a tiny lump under the lower left tip of star 2. There are several heavy lumps at star 11. A very heavy one touches the tip of the left center point, and another from the right center point to the dentils. There is another heavy lump between the lower right point and the dentils. A faint crack connects the bottoms of 180. There are clash marks at the bottom of the date.

REVERSE A-5, 6, 5, 7—used on **B1** and **B2**. T2 (first T in STATES) is sharply doubled. There are clash marks behind ES OF. The bases of the third feather from the top of the right wing and AME are heavily connected. There are lumps between the tail feathers and the right claw, and another heavy lump at dentils left of tail feathers.

Rarity 5

B2

OBVERSE 2—used on **B2**, **B3**, and **B12**. R in LIBERTY is doubled. Crack from the dentils left of 1 runs up towards the lowest curl. Star 8 is very close to the right top of Y. A small crack runs from the lower left point of star 8 toward the lower center point.

REVERSE A-5, 6, 5, 7. See description of **B1**. Usually weak on right wing of eagle.

Rarity 7

B3

OBVERSE 2—used on **B2**, **B3**, and **B12**. See description of **B2**.

REVERSE B-5, 5, 5, 6—used only on **B3**. There is a large group of cracks and small lumps in the center of the open space below IT in UNITED.

Rarity 6

B4

OBVERSE 4—used only on **B4**. A heavy crack runs from the outer edge of the coin left of base of 1 through the left tip of base up through the center of the top of 1 up slightly to the right into the back of the bust. Another crack from the dentils between stars 12 and 13 runs through star 12—where it forms a curve up towards the chin, then down to the middle of the neck.

REVERSE D-4, 5, 5, 7—used on **B4**, **B16**, and **B20**. T1 (in UNITED) is doubled at the base, and the upper right serif is very long. On the obverse the bust is swelling. Since there is not enough in the planchet to fill the raised bust, the coin is very weak on the reverse behind the bust. The last cloud and the upper right wing are very weak, as is cloud 8. The eagle has both the upper and lower beaks touching star 12.

Rarity 4

B5

OBVERSE 6—used on **B5** and **B8**. There is a small but sharp lump over the right serif of the upright of R. A fine crack from the center of star 5, up through stars 6 and 7, to the tops of LIB, to the rim over right side of B. A tiny crack from the rim curves down to the top of E.

REVERSE F-4, 5, 4, 5—used on **B5** and **B10**. There is a strong dot over the left side of the left serif of T3, the second T in States. A heavy line on cloud 4 (from the left) toward the tip of the right serif of T3.

Die State a: OBVERSE cracked from star 5, star 6, star 7, tops of LIB.

Die State b: Additional crack from the dentils, down through the right side of B, down to the top of the head.

Rarity 4

Note: Bolender says that **B6** is only a worn specimen of **B5**, and that **B7** is a late state of **B5**. Both **B6** and **B7** are not listed.

B8

OBVERSE 6, used on **B5** and **B8**. According to Bolender and Bowers, the obverse of **B8** is the same as the obverse of **B5**. Comparing the two varieties, this seems to be correct. The lump in the bottom of R seems to match, but it does seem to be slightly larger on **B8**. When you check the cracks, however, the picture changes a little. On both of my **B5**s there is a crack from the center of star 5 up to the left through star 6, near the top of star 7, through the tops of LIB, curving up to the dentils over the right side of B. This crack is the same on states a and b. On state b, in addition, there is a heavy vertical crack from the rim down through the right side of B to the hair just left of the curls on the top of the head.

None of these cracks appear on **B8**. Everything else seems to be the same on both **B5** and **B8**. It is easy to say that **B8** is an early die state before the cracks formed on **B5**. However, **B8** has its own devices. Heavy vertical lines appear above both sides of star 4. A heavy horizontal crack floats between the dentils and star 7 and L. If these cracks came before the ones on **B5**, they should still be seen on **B5**, which is not the case. Some other things on **B8**, but not on **B5**, are tiny lumps around stars 12 and 13.

REVERSE E-4, 5, 5, 6—used only on **B8**. There is a crack from below the center of A2 up through MER, where it turns up to the rim. A2 touches the third feather, and practically sits on the fourth feather.

Rarity 3

Note: Haseltine listed **B9** as **B8** with letters bifurcated. Bolender did not list it as a variety, and it is not listed here

B10

OBVERSE 7—used on **B10** and **B11**. In an attempt to curve the date, the 8 seems low and the 0s, especially the second one, are too high. There are some weak cracks and lumps near stars 12 and 13, and from the bust to the rim. The curl under E is not complete.

REVERSE F-4, 5, 4, 5—used on B5 and **B10**. There are many lumps:

1-Heavy lump, with a stem, on the left tip of the banner.

2-There are several lumps between the left tip of the banner and the wing feathers, down to just above the arrow heads.

3-There are several lumps between the left tail feathers and S1, with one lump inside the top of S1.

4-Some lumps are at the top of T2, and between T2 and A1.

5-There are lumps left of the center of T3, and a heavy lump between the tops of A1 and T3, with others left of the center of T3.

6-There is one small lump at the bottom of over the center of O. There are heavy lumps between O and F, with others between F and the tail feathers.

Die State a: reverse lumps but no cracks.

Die State b:

1-Crack from rim left of arrow feathers, left bottom of U1, arrow tips.

2-Crack from rim over center of N1, tops of ITED to rim over left wing tip.

3-Crack over top of T2.

4-Crack from right top of T2 down over cloud 2, 2 right points of star 2 - to star 8.

5-Crack 4 is crossed by crack 5, which runs from stars 3 to 8.

6-Crack from tip of top feather on right to dentils.

7-Heavy crack from star 10 - star 11 - across right wing.

8-Crack from center of A - top of M - dentils over E.

9-Crack from top of right end of banner curves up through center of bottom of E, center of R - top of I.

10-Heavy crack from rim splits into two cracks. The upper one goes through the left side of C across two leaves, to the second feather from the shield. The lower crack splits off down through the C just right of center across the leaves under CA. A third crack splits from the first crack in 10 down to the center outside berry.

Rarity 2

B11

OBVERSE 7—used on **B10** and **B11**. See description of **B10**.

REVERSE G-5, 5, 4, 6—used on **B11** and **B19**. The well-known AMERICAI variety. A heavy vertical crack appears after AMERICA, looking somewhat like an "I". All six of the upper row of stars touch the clouds above, and star 12 touches the lower beak.

Rarity 4

B12
OBVERSE 2—used on **B2**, **B3**, and **B12**. See description of **B2**.

REVERSE C-4, 4, 3, 5—used only on **B12**. A heavy bar, about 1 mm long, runs from the dentils left of U down to the right toward the left top of U. A series of dots appear in E1 (in UNITED), most of them in the left bottom of E, and two tiny dots in the right center of E. A large triangular lump outside of E3 (in AMERICA), above the lower left serif.

Die State a: As described above.

Die State b: Reverse cracked at top of OF, and right wing tip.

Rarity 3

B13
Note: B13 includes Haseltine and Bolender's **B18**. The dollars called **B18** turned out to be only die states of **B13**.

OBVERSE 9—used only on **B13**, including what was called **B18**. The high waves of the hair, under the right side of the upright of E and under the center of R, are very strong. The 8 in the date is larger than the 1, extending both above and below the 1.

REVERSE H-5, 5, 4, 6—used only on **B13** (although dies with the same numbers, but not the same dies, were used on **B11** and **B19**, and on **B14**). A2 is connected to the 3rd and 4th feathers, and to the base of M.

Die State a:

OBVERSE—perfect. **REVERSE**—a lumpy line is near the dentils and the right wing feathers.

Die State b:

OBVERSE—clash marks can be seen above the date.

REVERSE—clash mark of the bust, from star 4, cloud 7, F, right wing tip is strong. Another, heavier, line from star 5 touches clouds 7 and 8. Clash marks touch all of the stars on the left except star 1. Clash marks connect A2 to the wing feathers, and the tail feathers to the stem.

Die State c:

OBVERSE—a heavy crack from star 1, right of stars 2 and 3, the inner tip of star 4. A matching crack on the right side of the reverse, runs from star 8, left of stars 9 and 10, to the tip of star 11.

REVERSE—there are now six clash marks through the clouds, all from the clashing of the bust. There is a strong crack up through the shield, between M and E, to the rim.

Die State d:

OBVERSE—a heavy rim break covers stars 2 and 3, and a lighter one goes from star 8 to star 11. The second break causes the **REVERSE** to be weak at RI.

Rarity 3

B14

OBVERSE 10, used only on **B14**. There are six strong dots under, in and over the first O. There are other dots, smaller, between the 8 and the first 0, over the second O, and to the right, with two touching the bottom of the bust.

REVERSE I-5, 5, 4, 6—used only on **B14**. Star 12 touches both the upper and lower beaks. There are many lumps around the clouds, at the tops of clouds 2, 3, 4, 6 and 7. There are defects at the bottoms of clouds 2, 3, between 3 and 4, under clouds 5 and 6, and between clouds 7 and 8.

Die State a: No cracks on either the obverse or the reverse.

Die State b: Obverse cracks at both 0s in the date, the bust, and stars 1, 2, and 3.

Rarity 2

B15

OBVERSE 11—used only on **B15**. Star 13 almost touches the bust at the meeting of the drapery and the bust, the distance between the two being less than 1/2mm. The top of the 1 is even closer to the lowest curl. Star 1 is about 4mm from the nearest curl. There is a small dot between R and T.

REVERSE J-4, 5, 5, 6—used only on **B15**. The two outside arrowheads of the three top ones and one other arrowhead have no shafts. There are many small lumps—between N1 and I1, right of D1, under D1, between wing feathers and dentils, several right of S2, around R, I, C, and A. The left foot of M is resting on the top of the right foot of A. There are lumps around stars 1, 2, 3, and 4.

Rarity 3

B16

OBVERSE 5—used only on **B16**. There is a strong dot, level with the top of the curl under E, in line with the left side of E. A heavy flaw from just below the right top of R becomes weaker as it touches the left top of T. The tip of 1 in the date almost touches the lowest curl.

REVERSE D-4, 5, 5, 7—used on **B4**, **B16** and **B20**. T1, in UNITED, is heavily doubled at the bottom. There are many defects over UNITED. There are many heavy lumps over ES to the rim near O. The upper and lower beaks and star 12 all touch.

Rarity 2

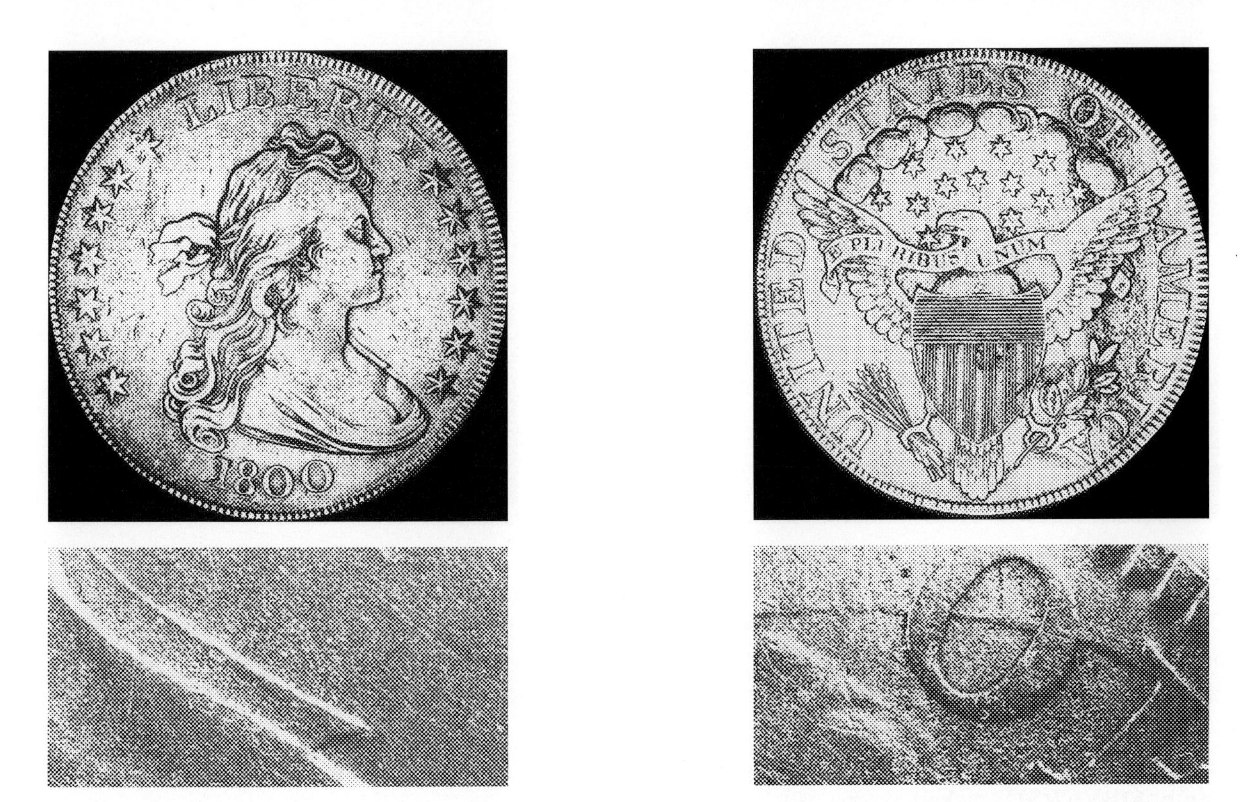

B17

Note: B17 of 1800 is the most difficult dollar in the series to study. According to Bolender, every known **B17** of 1800 has a collar on the neck from slightly above the throat to half way to the drapery. I have one with no collar and one with a collar. See photos.

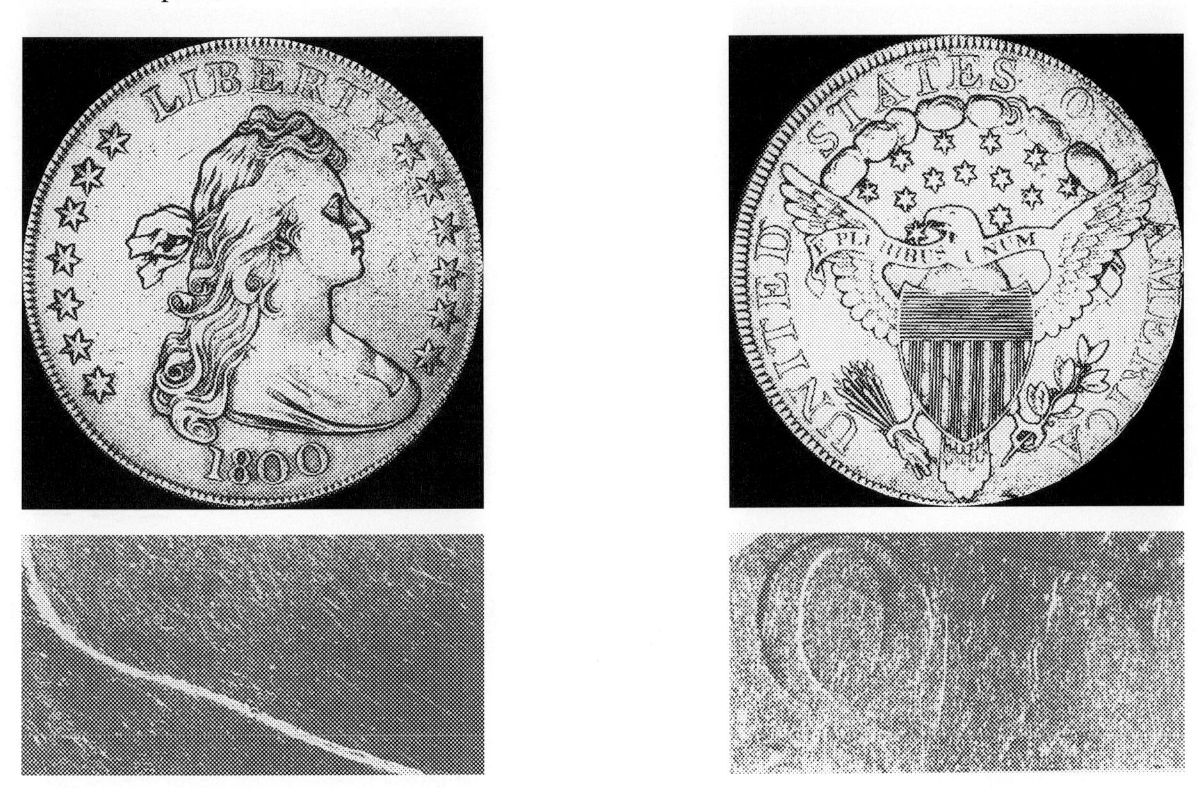

B17A

Rarity 3

Note: B18 is now believed to be a clashed die state of **B13**.

B19

OBVERSE 8—used only on **B19**. 1 in the date almost touches the lowest curl. Clash marks run through the top of the date. Clash marks from the tail of the eagle touch the top of and R. Clash marks from the sides of the eagle's tail show at the left sides of E and R.

REVERSE G-5, 5, 4, 6—used on **B11** and **B19**. A very heavy vertical line right of A3 causes this to be known as the AMERICAI variety. See description of **B11**.

Die State a: Obverse and reverse perfect. Dies clashed.

Die State b: OBVERSE cracked at tops of LIBE.

Die State c: REVERSE cracked at border above U.

Rarity 2

B20

OBVERSE 3—used only on **B20**. Star 8 is very close to the Y, about 1/3mm. The bottom is about 1/2mm from the Y. These are very similar to the dies used on the 1804 dollars, and **B20**'s have been altered to make counterfeit 1804 dollars. There are elongated dentils, which look like dentils with spikes coming from the bottom at stars 4, 5, and 6. Faint cracks come out of stars 2, 3, 4, 5, 6, 7, 10 and 12.

REVERSE D-4, 5, 5, 7—used on **B4**, **B16**, and **B20**. T1 is doubled at the bottom, and the top right serif of T1 is elongated. The point of star 12 is heavily connected to both the upper and lower beaks of the eagle. There are several lumps in STATES in the tops of ES, and halfway to the top of O.

Rarity 6

Chapter Eight:

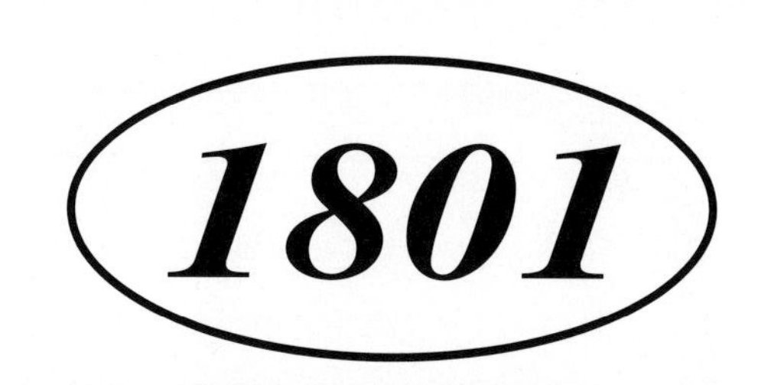

Rapid Finder For 1801

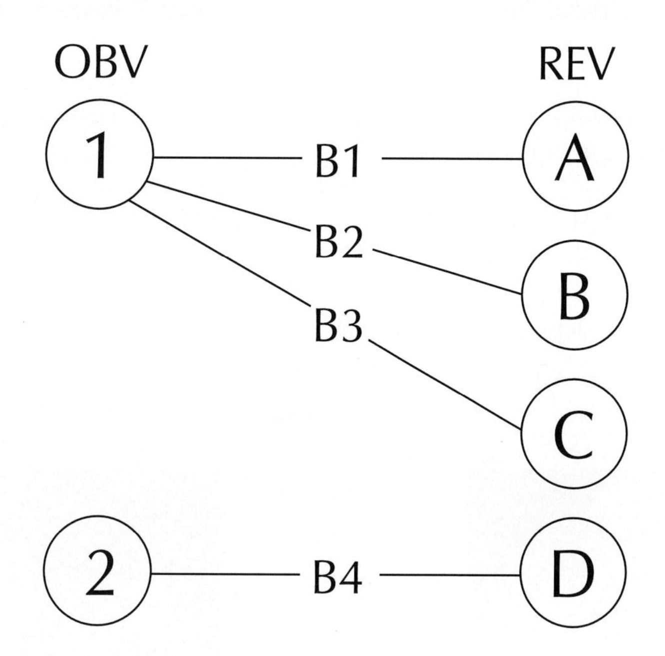

SEE APPENDIX A FOR LOCATION NUMBERS

Appendix No.	Bolender No.	Description
3434	B2	**REVERSE** B - The high center point of cloud 3 touches both inner serifs of A1.
	B2	**OBVERSE** 1 - A clash mark forms a "collar" from the throat to about halfway along the bust.
3556	B4	**REVERSE** D - A sharp point from the curve of D near the bottom points to the second feather from the bottom.
	B4	**OBVERSE** 2 - There is a lump under the center of the lowest curl.
3556	B3	**REVERSE** C - The lower right serifs of all three T's are missing.
		OBVERSE 3 - There are small lumps around the left tops of E and R.
5545	B1	**REVERSE** A - Cloud 3 touches the left foot of A. On later examples there are heavy clash marks.
	B1	**OBVERSE** 1, used on B1, B2, and B3.
	B5	Proof restrike 1801.

B1

OBVERSE 1, used on **B1**, **B2**, and **B3**. Star 1 is 2mm from curl 2. Star 7 is 1.5mm from bottom of L. Y is about .75mm from Star 8. Star 13 is 1.5mm from the bust.

REVERSE A-5, 5, 4, 5—used on **B1** only. Cloud 3 touches left foot of A1.

Die State a: Obverse perfect, reverse perfect.

Die State b: Crack from rim, down through STA, clouds 3, 4, 5, 6, 7, 8, right wing tips, AM.

Die State c: Swelling causes heavy lump at bottom of ME to upright of R. Clash marks on obverse and reverse, but not through O.

Rarity 3

B2

OBVERSE 1, used on **B1**, **B2**, and **B3**. See description of **B1**. **B2** has a "collar" on the top of the bust and bottom of the neck, really a clash mark.

REVERSE B-3, 4, 3, 4—used on **B2** only. There is a strong crack from the second feather on the left wing - up to the dentils. A clash mark of the obverse bust runs through OF.

Rarity 3

B3

OBVERSE 1, used on **B1**, **B2**, and **B3**. See description of **B1**. The crack to the left from the bottom of 1 is quite strong.

REVERSE C-3, 5, 5, 6 used on **B3** only. The lower right serifs are missing on all 3 Ts. There are many small lumps right of S2.

Rarity 3

B4

OBVERSE 2—used only on **B4**. There is a lump under the center of the lowest curl. There is another lump between stars 5 and 6. The first 1 in the date practically touches the lowest curl.

REVERSE D-3, 5, 5, 6—used only on **B4**. A sharp point from the right side of D, below the center, points to the fourth feather from the top of the left wing. The left bottom serifs of all three T's are longer than the right bottom serifs.

Rarity 4

Note: B5, 5, 5, 5, 6 is a proof restrike.

Chapter Nine:

Rapid Finder For 1802

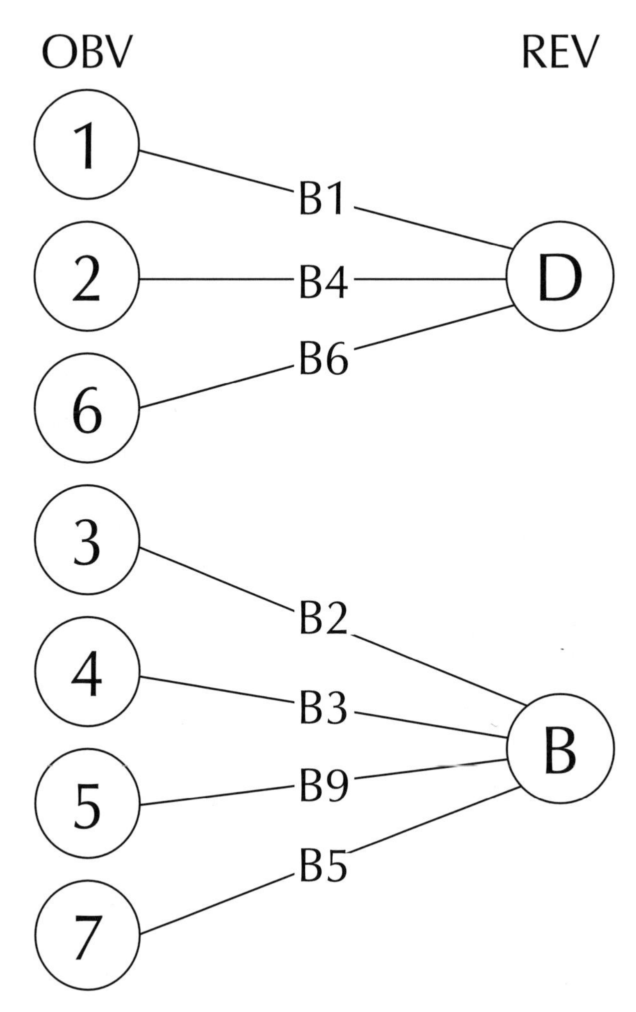

SEE APPENDIX A FOR LOCATION NUMBERS

Appendix No.	Bolender No.	Description
3434	B1 - B4	
	B6	**REVERSE** A—heavy line from dentils to second feather from the top on left side of reverse. Point of star 12 is a tiny bit inside, past the upper beak. It is so close to the beak that I call it a 3.
	B1	**OBVERSE** 1—the 2 in the date is over a 1. Some heavy clash marks cause a heavy diagonal section to form at the throat, and a smaller one where the bust meets the neck. There is another clash mark below the ribbon on the back of the head. The 8 is doubled at the left side of the upper loop.
	B4	**OBVERSE** 2—the 2 in the date is over a 1. The tip of the 1 touches the lowest curl. The 8 is doubled at the left side of both the upper and the lower loops, with the lower one being stronger.
	B6	**OBVERSE** 6—the 2 is not over any other number. The 8 is perfect, with no doubling. In LIBERTY, the lower right serif of T is missing.
3556	B2 - B3	
	B5 - B9	**REVERSE** B—sharp point down to the right from the right side of D, below the center. The left bottom serifs of all 3 Ts on each of the four varieties are longer than the right bottom serifs.
	B2	**OBVERSE** 3—the 2 in the date is over a 1. The horizontal tip of the 1 is over the left side of the 2.
	B3	**OBVERSE** 4—the 2 in the date is over a 1. There is a heavy lump in the field between stars 8 and 9, and closer to the stars than to the forehead.
	B5	**OBVERSE** 7—the numbers 1802 in the date start fairly high, almost touching the lowest curl, and each digit of the 1802 is higher than the last, with the 2 close to the bottom of the bust.
	B9	**OBVERSE** 5—the 2 in the date is over a 1. There is a fairly large smooth lump under the right side of B, and slightly left of the tip of the curl under B.
	B8	Proof Restrike

1802/1

B1

OBVERSE 1—2 over 1, used only on **B1**. The left side of the upright of 1 is in the center of 2. The top of 1 is slightly higher than the top of the 2. The left top of the 8 is doubled. A clash mark runs diagonally across the throat from the underside of the chin to the center of the neck.

REVERSE A-3, 4, 3, 4—used on **B1**, **B4**, and **B6**. The upper right serifs of all 3 Ts are longer than the upper left serifs. A heavy crack connects the second feather from the top of the left wing up to the right to the dentils. Two small dots are under M.

Rarity 4

B2

OBVERSE 3—2 over 1, used only on **B2**. Right side of 1 is under the center of the 2 in the date. The point of the top of 1 is over the lower left serif of the 2, and the top of the 2 is just above the top of the 1. Star 7 is 1.5mm from the L, and star 8 is 1.25mm from the Y. Star 13 is less than 0.5mm from the bust.

REVERSE B-3, 5, 5, 6—used on **B2**, **B3**, **B5**, and **B9**. A sharp point from the right side of D points to the fourth feather from the top on the left wing tip. The left lower serif of all 3 Ts is longer than the right lower serif.

Rarity 3

B3

OBVERSE 4—2 over 1, used only on **B3**, 2/1, with the top of the 1 slightly above the 2. The upright of the 1 is slightly right of center. The section above the diagonal of 2 is very thin, and the section below the diagonal is very thick. There is a heavy lump between the forehead and the space between stars 8 and 9. The distance between the lump and the forehead is double that of the distance between the lump and stars 8 and 9.

REVERSE B-3, 5, 5, 6—used on **B2**, **B3**, **B5**, and **B9**. See description of **B2**.

Rarity 3

B4

OBVERSE 2—2/1, used only on **B4**. The top of the 1 under the two is slightly higher than the top of the 2. The 1 in the date strongly touches the lowest curl. Both loops of the 8 are doubled on the left side, with the doubling being sharper on the lower loop. Star 7 is 1.5mm from the L, and star 8 is 1mm from the Y. Star 13 is .25mm from the drapery on the bust.

REVERSE A-3, 4, 3, 4-See description of **B1**.

Rarity 4

B5

OBVERSE 7—used only on **B5**. Unfortunately, this is one of the best made obverses, making it very difficult to identify. Everything is nicely spaced. The date does run uphill, with the 1 slightly below center and almost touching the lowest curl. The 1 is about 2.5mm from the bust, but the last digit, the 2, is very close to the bottom of the bust, less than .5mm.

REVERSE B-3, 5, 5, 6—used on **B2**, **B3**, **B5**, and **B9**. See description of **B2**.

Rarity 5

B6

OBVERSE 6—used only on **B6**. The lower right serif of T is missing. The date runs slightly uphill, but the 2 is a full mm from the bottom of the bust.

REVERSE A-3, 4, 3, 4—used on **B1**, **B4**, and **B6**. See description of **B1**.

Rarity 1
Note: Haseltine's **B7** is the same as **B6**.
Note: **B8** is a proof restrike.

B9

OBVERSE 5, used only on **B9** 2 over 1. There is a heavy lump under B. Star 7 is 2mm from L. Star 8 is 1.5mm from Y. Star 13 is .5mm from the bust.

REVERSE B-3, 5, 5, 6—used on **B2**, **B3**, **B5** and **B9**. See description of **B2**.

Die State a: As above.

Die State b: Obverse cracked from over 1, over 8, top of 0, bottom of two dentils right of 2. There is a die crack from the bust to the rim.

Die State c: Two cracks, rim to star 13 into field.

Rarity 5

Chapter Ten:

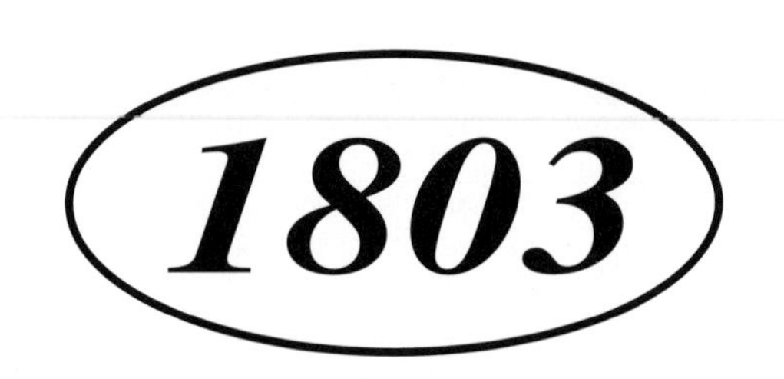

Rapid Finder For 1803

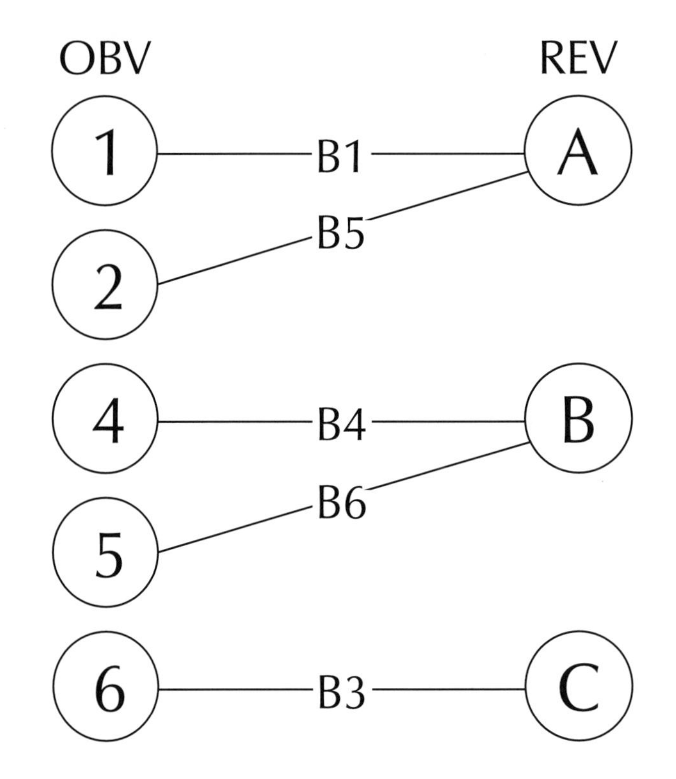

SEE APPENDIX A FOR LOCATION NUMBERS

REVERSE B Bolender lists B2, B4, and B6 as having a common reverse, which he calls reverse a. Bowers calls the same three varieties reverse b, stating our comments that B2 may not exist. Walter Breen told me years ago that, in his opinion, it did not exist. I have not seen one, and have mentioned in later editions of Bolender that B2 probably did not exist.

Appendix No.	Bolender No.	Description
3434	B4 and B6	**REVERSE** B—twelve arrowheads. B4 has a weak line from the rim to the top feather of the left wing, and a heavy line to the feather below. On B6 both of these lines are very heavy. Another rather heavy vertical line on B6 is right of the D, with several lines from the left top of D to the dentils. The three dentils over D have joined together and dropped closer to the top of D.
	B4	**OBVERSE** 4—the 1 touches the lowest curl. All of the other varieties are very close, but none touches. The top of the 3 is very long, at a steep angle, and close to the bottom loop of the 3.
	B6	**OBVERSE** 5—3 is double struck at the left bottom. A line from the upper right point of star 7 runs up to the left of top of L.
3556	B1 and B5	**REVERSE** A—twelve very nice arrowheads, 3 of which have short stems. A thirteenth arrowhead is under the top right arrowhead. The 13th is very weak, with no shaft at all.
	B1	**OBVERSE** 1—small 3. A series of faint cracks starts at the rim over R, through the lower left serif of R, through the hair, just left of the 8.
	B5	**OBVERSE** 2 - Very small 3, smaller than the 3 on B1. Letters LIB are close to each other. Letters ERT are twice as far from each other. BE are quite distant from each other, as are TY.
5535	B3	**REVERSE** C—bottoms of AM touch, with the bottom of M being slightly higher than bottom of A. M, E almost touch. E-R 1/2mm, R-I 1/2mm; I-C 1-1/2 mm, C-A 1/2mm.
	B3	**OBVERSE** 6—star 8 is almost 2mm from Y.
5556	B7	Proof Restrike1803

B1

OBVERSE 1—used only on **B1**. Small 3. There is a crack down from the dentils through the two left serifs of R - between the two highest curls (under E and R). A second crack just left of the 8 up between the same two curls about 1/2mm right of the first crack, and it curves left to meet the first crack.

REVERSE A-3, 5, 5, 6—used on **B1** and **B5**. There is a weak point, down to the right, from the lower right side of D toward the fourth feather from the top of the left wing. All three T's have longer serifs on the right side of the top than on the left side.

Die State a: Obverse cracks as mentioned above.

Die State b: The area between the two cracks between the top of the hair and the bottom of the R - has broken loose as a cud.

Rarity 4

Note: I still believe that 1803 **B2** does not exist.

B3

OBVERSE 6—used only on **B3**. Small 3. The obverse is cracked around the bottom of 8, curving up between 1 and 8. Star 8 is almost 2mm from Y.

REVERSE C-5, 5, 3, 5—used only on **B3**. The upper right serifs of all three Ts are slightly longer than the left serifs.

Rarity 4

B4

OBVERSE 4—used on **B4** only. 3 is the same size as the other numbers in the date. 1 touches the lowest curl. Star 1 is 1mm from the second curl from the bottom. Star 7 is slightly over 2mm from the L. Star 8 is 1.5mm from the Y. Star 13 practically touches the drapery on the bust.

REVERSE B-3, 4, 3, 4—used on **B4** and **B6**. A heavy line connects the 2nd feather from the top - up to left to the dentils. The upper right serifs on the three Ts are longer than the left serifs.

Rarity 2

B5

OBVERSE 2—used only on **B5**. Small 3. The 1 is a little low, and the 3 is slightly high according to where they should be to have a nice alignment for the date. Star 1 is 1.75mm from curl 2. Star 7 is 1.5mm from the bottom of L. Star 8 is 1.25mm from the bottom of Y, and star 13 is about 0.75mm from the drapery on the bust. The upper right serif of T is longer than the upper left serif.

REVERSE A-3, 5, 5, 6—used on **B1** and **B5**. See description of **B1**.

Rarity 2

B6

OBVERSE 5—used only on **B6**. The 3 in the date is rather large, taller than the O. The top of the 3 is thick, and the left bottom of the 3 is heavily doubled.

REVERSE B-3, 4, 3, 4—used on **B4** and **B6**. **B4** was struck first, and the berries are strong, with full stems. On **B6** the berries are very small, and the stems are practically gone, with only traces remaining. **B4** has two medium lines from the left wing tip to the dentils. **B6** has two very heavy lines, and a third, a heavy vertical line just right of D, which is not on **B4**. **B6** has a heavy lump under the E in UNITED, which is not on **B4**.

Rarity 2

B7 is a proof restrike.

Early Silver Dollar Die Marriages Discovered Since the 1881 Haseltine Type Table—A Detailed Analysis

by W. David Perkins, NLG

Do you know how many new die marriages of early silver dollars (1794-1803) were discovered in 1997? How many years, prior to 1997, had it been since a new die marriage had been discovered and publicized? How many new die marriages have been discovered since M. H. *Bolender's The United States Silver Dollars from 1794 to 1803* was first published in 1950? Since the publication in 1881 of the *Haseltine Type Table?* Who discovered these marriages and when? When were they first reported?

Answering these questions is not easy. There is no one reference to turn to that has all the answers, and not all of the answers are straightforward or even published. Furthermore, there have been a number of "new discoveries" reported or cataloged over the years that turned out to be new die marriages. I imagine even a few early dollar specialists will be surprised at some of the answers! So write down your answers or guesses and read on…

The new Bowers-Borckardt (BB) numbers are courtesy of Mark Borckardt, Bowers & Merena and follow the numbering sequence employed in Q. David Bower's book, *Silver Dollars of the United States,* published in 1993. The new Bolender (B) numbers were assigned by Jules Reiver. These will be included in a revised edition of Bolender's book which will be published sometime in 1998.

1795 B-18: (Reported Discovery, later discredited and shown to be the same as 1795 B-6)

The B-18 (Bolender 18) number was first assigned by M. H. Bolender to a "discovery" he reported in *The Numismatist,* December, 1952, page 1176:

The first discovery of a new major variety of an early silver dollar before 1804 has recently been made, two years after the publication of Bolender's standard reference book on the subject which was published in July, 1950.

The credit for this new discovery goes to Frank M. Stirling, A.N.A. member 10052, of…Baton Rouge La., and the thrills of his finding, and pride of ownership are making his specialty most interesting. Mr. Stirling is one of the most active collectors in this field.

This 1795 dollar, to be known as Bolender No. 18, was struck from the rare obverse die as used for B-13. The reverse was struck from a newly made die with only three leaves in the wreath below the first S in STATES. Later, a fourth leaf was added to the die, and B-5, B-6, and B-12 coins were struck.

This coin will rate rarity 8, as it is the only one known to me up to this time. When the book was published over two years ago, it was hoped that other new varieties would be brought to light. Some minor sub-varieties have appeared and always will as there are so many different states of dies, such as die cracks and their degrees of progress, extent of bifurcations, and peculiarities of striking. But a new die, or a new combination of obverse and reverse dies, constitutes a major variety and the constant search for things of this kind in any series keeps collectors forever young.

M. H. Bolender, ANA 2776

San Marino, California

Bolender's announcement included a photo of both the obverse and reverse of the Frank Stirling specimen of this reported new variety. Unfortunately, this "new die combination" turned out to be just a different die state of 1795 B-6 (BB-25).

The B-18 number being assigned and later dropped is the source of much confusion in the rare, high numbered die marriages of 1795 dollars. The next variety discovered became B-19, then was later changed to B-18, B-20 became B-19, etc. This will become clear as you read on. [For example, when this B-18 was later dropped, the Eliasberg B-19 (see below) became the B-18. Furthermore, another specimen of this erroneous B-18 was offered as part of an extensive variety collection formed by W. Earl Spies and sold by Stack's at public auction in December, 1974 (both obverse and reverse were plated in this catalog). One might think that the 1795 B-18 is known by multiple specimens, which today is not the case].

1795 B-18 (BB-17): (Referred to as B-19 by specialists at the time of its discovery)

This die marriage was discovered by Walter Breen in the Eliasberg Collection and was reported in the July, 1953 *The Numismatist,* page 706. The obverse was that of 1795 B-7 married to a new reverse die. This specimen remained in the Eliasberg collection until it was sold in April, 1997. It was formerly in the Clapp and Earle collections, unattributed in these sales as to the variety. (For more information see "Possibly Unique 1795 B-18 Dollar Variety Soon to be Offered?" in the John Reich Journal, Volume 10, issue 2, April, 1996 pages 34-35).

This specimen was offered by Bowers & Merena in the *Louis E. Eliasberg, Sr. Collection Sale,* April, 1997 as lot 2168. It was graded EF-45. Cataloging of this lot was comprehensive and encompassed two full pages. Included were extra large photos of both the obverse and reverse, along with a color plate (normal size). Also included was a detailed description of the new reverse die, pedigree, and other pertinent information. It realized $52,800 in very competitive bidding.

Today the Eliasberg specimen, now in the collection of a New Jersey early dollar specialist collector, remains unique. No other specimens are known to this author.

1795 B-19 (BB-19): (Called B-20 when discovered, later changed to B-19)

This die marriage was formed when the obverse die of B-2 was mated to the reverse die of B-7. Per a letter to Jules Reiver from Frank Stirling, published in *The Lettered Edge* (Newsletter of the Bust Dollar Club, Fall 1978), March 11, 1978, "The B-20 dollar was found in the late Maurice Finman's collection, Pensacola, Fla. in the late 1950s. I have the coin, Earl Spies and Mr. and Mrs. Ostheimer have seen it and OK'd the variety. It has never been published."

Thus this die marriage was known to at least a few specialists prior to 1960. It is unknown if Mr. Stirling ever reported it to Bolender. Stirling may have reported it as it is included in the *1974 Silver Anniversary Edition of Valuation List For The United States Early Silver Dollars from 1974 to 1803* by M. H. Bolender. (The list had Bolender's name on it, but it was published by Bebee's Inc., Omaha). The valuation listing was for "1795 B-16 to 20." (For more information on this variety see *John Reich Journal,* Volume 10/ Issue 2, pages 16-17.)

1975 B-20 (BB-16): (Called B-21 in the February 12, 1972 Lester Merkin Sale)

This die marriage was catalogued as being "identified" by Walter Breen. Most likely it was Breen who discovered this marriage of two known dies. The discovery specimen appeared in the February 12, 1972 Lester Merkin *Public Auction Sale,* lot 299. The catalog description read:

*1795 **"B-21".** New muling of known dies. Obv. B-7, Rev. **B-8,** but finer than the Bolender plate coin of that variety. Immediately identified by straight, die scratch in field, like part of an extra A left of first A in AMERICA, pointing to the nearest berry; recut C in AMERICA. Just about VF, many obv. adjustment marks. Rev. sharper than the obv. and fully VF. The B-8 die was formerly known only by two impressions of that variety; the present muling is superior to either of them and in addition represents a discovery linking the B-8 dies with the remainder of the group (Bolender 16, 10 , 17, 1, 2, 7, 19, 18, 12, 5 and 6). Identified by Walter Breen, originally obtained merely as a specimen of the date. Unpublished, to date **unique. ILLUST.***

From the plate, the coin appears to be at least Very Fine, possibly even Extremely Fine. The B-21 (now B-20) was purchased by specialist Frank Stirling from this sale for $900. Frank Stirling graded it VF+.

To the best of my knowledge, this specimen remained the only one known for twenty-five years. In mid January, 1998 (shortly after originally mailing this article to be published) a second example of B-20 was reported! I received a phone call from Mark Borckardt of Bowers & Merena on Tuesday, January 20, 1998 informing me that a dealer had attributed and sent to them a 1795 Flowing Hair dollar (correctly) attributed as B-20. A dealer had bought it unattributed, attributed it as B-20 (BB-16) and had sent it to B&M to verify attribution. The unfortunate news was that this specimen, although it graded VF or so, was holed. Regardless, it is only the second specimen of the die marriage known. Collectors will soon have a chance to acquire this rare die marriage as it is consigned to the May, 1998 Bowers & Merena auction sale.

1795 B-21 (BB-28):

This new die marriage turned up in 1997. I first learned of its existence in April, 1997. I received a phone call that a new die marriage of the 1795 dollar had been discovered. It was to be offered in the June 3, 1997 Spink America auction sale of *Important Coins and Banknotes, Including Colonial and United States Coinage and Medals, formerly the stock of Burdette G. Johnson of St. Louis, Missouri.* There was little pre-sale publicity for this important find. The May 27, 1997 issue of *Numismatic News,* page 35 contained in their "Auctions" column the following: "1796 coinage highlights Spink America auction." Under a section labeled "Dollars" this new early dollar marriage was mentioned for the first time publicly: "1795 Two Leaves with reverse die of Bolender-16 and a previously unrecorded obverse die, F to VF, $10,000-$15,000." Ads in both *Coin World* (May 19, 1997) and *Numismatic News* (May 20, 1997) mentioned under "Silver Coins Include:" that "Dollars include a new and unrecorded obverse die for a 1795 coupled with a B-16 reverse..." This specimen was catalogued in the May sale as:

[Lot] 186 1795, two leaves (Bolender-obverse die unlisted, reverse

die of B-16), obverse scratches, fine to very fine, of considerable importance to the specialist collector of early silver Dollars $10,000-$15,000.

The coin was plated—both obverse and reverse—in black and white. The lot realized $23,100. Prior to the sale I called to inquire about the lot. I requested a photocopy of the B. G. Johnson (2x2) envelope in which the coin had been stored. This proved extremely interesting. Typed on the front of the envelope was: "Not in Haseltine/Head of 1794/Very good/excessively rare/$60.00/ mxco/BGJ". Thus this die marriage was discovered and known to B. G. Johnson probably in the middle to late 1930s, and for sure prior to publication of Bolender's book in 1950! (The reference "not in Haseltine" refers to the *Haseltine Type Table,* first published in 1881, which was the standard reference for attributing early dollar varieties prior to Bolender's work.) This coin lay in a bank vault, correctly identified as a new variety, and remained unknown to specialists (for reasons not known) for over fifty years!

1795 B-22 (BB-29):

The most recent discovery is another new die marriage of the 1795 dollar. This marriage turned up in October, 1997 in a group of twenty early dollars sent to ANACS for attribution, grading, and encapsulation. The discovery was told on the front page of *Coin World,* November 3, 1997. According to Paul Gilkes' article, "ANACS grader Charles Erb was the first grader to inspect the discovery coin. After examining the coin for several minutes, Erb determined that the coin did not exactly match any of the coins in any of the ANACS early dollar references. ANACS senior numismatist Michael Fahey confirmed the coin was an unlisted variety, struck from a known obverse die, but a previously unknown reverse die." The coin was graded "net Fine-12" due to some tooling apparent on the obverse. The coin was shipped to Mark Borckardt at Bowers & Merena for verification. Borckardt assigned the BB-29 number to this new discovery. The number Bolender-22 was assigned to this marriage by Jules Reiver. The obverse is the same as B-12 (BB-26). The new reverse die was described in *Coin World* by Mark Borckard as:

Three leaves under each wing of eagle. There are six berries in each branch, a feature which is diagnostic among the three leaves type. The left branch has a vertical pair of berries below the left edge of the first S in STATES. There is only one berry on the left branch of the wreath between the eagle's wing and ribbon bow, and it is on the inside of the wreath. The right branch has a berry directly below the center of M in AMERICA, and two berries inside the wreath below the wing.

The coin's obverse and reverse appeared in *Coin World* on page 1. This specimen quickly found a home in a prominent specialist's collection.

1796 B-6 (BB-64):

It is unknown when this die marriage was discovered. Most likely it was in the 1950s after the publication of Bolender's book. Two specimens are known to me, both of which can be traced to the middle to late 1950s.

Early dollar specialist K. P. Austin acquired a specimen privately in June, 1957 from Walter Breen. Most likely it was Breen who discovered this new marriage. (But for some reason Breen did not publish the discovery as he had done in 1953 for the new 1795 B-18 variety.) A. J. Ostheimer, an early dollar specialist with an extensive variety collection, acquired this specimen from Mr. Austin. It was later resold as lot 823 (plated) in Superior's *1975 ANA Auction Sale*. This specimen now resides in the Jules Reiver collection. (Note also that this specimen is the plate coin in the Bowers' silver dollar book.)

A second example of the B-6 was in the collection of Emanuel Taylor, another early dollar specialist. It is unknown when or where Taylor acquired this coin. The Taylor collection was acquired by the Kagins in the late 1950s and was offered in a little known catalog titled *AMERICA'S OUTSTANDING COLLECTION OF SILVER DOLLARS For Sale at Fixed Prices.* The catalog was probably issued around 1959. It was not dated. Lot 19 (unfortunately not plated) was described as follows:

1796 NEW MAJOR VARIETY, Obverse B-2, Reverse NEW DIE with die break vertically bisecting the right third, very fine except that the right third is virtually uncirculated with mint luster. A most interesting coin which helps explain why some come in two different degrees of condition. UNIQUE......$1,250.00.

Bolender was aware of this die marriage in 1956 because it was included in his *New 1956 Revised Edition of Valuation List Of The United States Early Silver Dollars from 1794-1803.* (For some reason the 1796 B-6 was not included on the 1974 valuation list.) I also believe Breen was aware of both of these (B-6) specimens. According to Art Kagin, Breen worked for the Kagins around this time. Breen most likely viewed the Taylor-Kagin specimen. For sure he was aware of the fixed price list of the Taylor collection. To my knowledge the 1956 Bolender Valuation List is the first mention in print of the 1796 B-6. The Kagin FPL is the first time a specimen of this die marriage was publicly offered for sale.

This specimen of 1796 B-6 was hidden away until it reappeared as lot 1249 in the September 11-13, 1995 Bowers & Merena *The Greenwald and Jackson Collections Sale.* It was plated (enlarged photo) for the first time, and sold for $36,300 with three collectors competing for the lot as it passed $30,000! The winner was "Mr. 1796." The coin has been displayed as part of his "1796 Die Study-Year Set" at the ANA summer conventions recently in Denver (1996) and New York City (1997). I believe that this and the Taylor-Kagin specimen are the same.

1798 B-32 (BB-91):

This new muling of the 1798 B-1 obverse and the B-4 reverse die was discovered by W. G. "Farish" Baldenhofer and was reported to readers of *The Numismatist* in a June, 1957 article, on page 651 (with obverse and reverse photos included). Farish Baldenhofer was an early dollar specialist and was quite active in the 1950s. Frank Stirling authored the article at Mr. Baldenhofer's request:

A new major variety of an early silver dollar before 1804 has been discovered. This is the fourth major variety known to have been discovered since the publication of M. H. Bolender's standard reference book on the subject in July, 1950. The credit goes to W. G. Baldenhofer, A.N.A. No. 14664, Springfield, Ohio, one of the foremost collectors in this field.

The new variety was struck from a combination of the obverse die as used for B-1 with the reverse die B-4, a muling heretofore unknown. On this specimen the sixth and seventh stars and the L in LIBERTY are weak due to the damaged condition of the dies at the time of striking. The corresponding portion of the reverse at the letters UN of UNITED is also weak. Short die cracks show on the obverse; one from center of 9 through top part of 8 to bust, another from edge of bust downward to border, and a third from the lowest point of thirteenth star downward to border. Part of the lowest curl and most of the second curl from the bottom are missing but this is a characteristic of the B-1 die. The long stems connecting the two lowest berries on the right side of the olive branch probably is the feature that most easily distinguishes the B-4 reverse die from all others. Bolender has examined this dollar and has numbered the variety "B-32." It will rate Rarity 8.

The publication of Mr. Bolender's excellent book on the early dollars, with plates, laid the groundwork for creating great interest in this series. Specialists are now carefully examining these interesting old dollars at every opportunity in hope of finding unpublished varieties, sub-varieties, or one that is excessively rare. It would be most interesting to have all such discoveries recorded in The Numismatist *as was done in the case of the 1795 B-18, December, 1952, page 1176, and the 1795 B-19, July, 1953, page 706.*

The Baldenhofer "discovery" specimen was later sold privately to dollar specialist A. J. Ostheimer. It was offered as lot 853: "Unlisted and Heretofore Unpublished 1798" in the August, *1975 A.N.A. Auction Sale* by Superior Stamp and Coin Co., conservatively graded as Fine-15 where it realized a very strong $1,300. This same specimen reappeared as lot 472 in Superior Galleries' *The Dr. Donald Davenport Collection* sale, February 21 & 22, 1977 where it was acquired by Jules Reiver.

It should be mentioned that the number B-32 (or H-32, the Haseltine equivalent number) has been applied to specimens that catalogers did not attribute correctly as existing varieties or sub-varieties. A 1798 dollar called H-32 in the Numismatic Gallery sale of the *World's Greatest Collection of United States Silver Coins,* January 20, 1945 is an example. It is described as "Large eagle and knobless 9..." The correct B-32 obverse has a knob 9 in the date. A specimen, lot 110, in the *W. Earl Spies Collection Sale*, Stack's, 1974 was called B-32 also. The obverse was that of B-6, the reverse B-17. This combination is the same as the B-6 die marriage described in Bolender. Thus the "Spies B-32" is not and was not a new die marriage.

1798 B-33 (BB-117):

This new die marriage was discovered by Mulford B. Simons of Penn Valley Rare Coins in January, 1973. Mulford B. Simons acquired the dollar and was unable to successfully attribute the coin according to Bolender variety. He took the coin to Wilmington, Delaware specialist Jules Reiver for attribution. Jules determined it was the obverse of Bolender 26-31 with a new reverse! (Note the obverse die for 1798 B-33 was used in the striking of seven die marriages!) Jules numbered it B-33.

The discovery was reported in *Coin World,* April 25, 1973 by Jules Reiver and Mulford B. Simons as follows, "There is always something new in numismatics, if not under the sun, and a 1798 silver dollar with a hitherto unreported reverse is a case in point. It was authenticated by Mulford B. Simons of Pennsylvania, backed up by Jules Reiver of Delaware, and titled B-33." The article appeared on page 65 and was entitled "Discover New Reverse Design on 1798 U. S. Silver Dollar". It continued on describing the new die marriage, " Reiver adds that the lower reverse seems strong and that the die must have broken in two, as the upper and lower halves are not in the same plane."

Although the 1798 B-33 remains rare today, specialist W. Earl Spies was able to acquire two specimens prior to his collection being sold in December, 1974. The two specimens were different die states, one late and the other very late. Very few have been reported since. The specimen called H-33 in the *World's Greatest Collection,* lot 60, is not a B-33 as we know it today. And the following lot, called H-34 was most likely a B-8.

"Not in *Haseltine Type Table Catalog* of 1881":

There were five new varieties listed (that were not in the 1881 *Haseltine Type Table*) in M. H. Bolender's *The United States Early Silver Dollars from 1794-1803* when first published in 1950. They were 1795 B-16, B-17; 1798 B-31; 1800 B-20; and 1802/1 B-9.

The 1795 B-16 was acquired by Bolender around 1932. This "discovery specimen" of B-16 appeared in Bolender's February 23, 1952 *183rd Auction Sale* of his reference collection of early dollars, lot 19:

1795 silver dollar. B-16. *New variety, not in Haseltine. Obverse from the same die as B-1 and B-10. The reverse is new in the arrangement of the berries and leaves in the wreath, and is described in my book. Uncirculated, with proof surface, a few trivial nicks visible under a glass. Beautifully toned, and a magnificent example, and one of the rarest of all dollars. Rarity 8, the only specimen known, and I believe it to be unique! Purchased by me at an Elder sale in New York 20 years ago. A prominent collector who was also in attendance bid against me, and it brought seven times the starting bid, and a new record for a 1795 dollar. The competition was the sensation of the entire auction sale. It is certainly worth more than any other dollar of this date. Plate. (Reverse of this coin was used for plate II in book.) $400.*

The lot was sold to specialist K. P. Austin for $440 on the $400 estimate. It is unclear from the Bolender catalog description who discovered it. Mr. Austin later sold it to A. J. Ostheimer. It was sold by Superior in the *1975 ANA Auction Sale.* This specimen was again offered in the Superior Galleries February, 1977 *The Dr. Donald Davenport* sale. Lot 468. Its whereabouts are unknown to me today.

The 1795 B-17 (new muling of known dies) that Bolender discovered and included in his 1950 book is not believed to exist by most specialists today. The coin Bolender called B-17 appeared as lot 220 in M. H. Bolender's November 29, *1932 Seventy Ninth Auction Sale...the Extensive Collection of Mr. P. C. Clark of Cleveland, Ohio.* In my opinion, the coin was misattributed by Bolender and likely was a 1795 B-10.

It is not known when or by whom the 1798 B-31 was discovered. Bolender had two specimens of this die marriage (lots 84 and 85 in his reference collection sale). Lot 84 was acquired from the Col. Green Collection. Lot 85 was acquired from St. Louis Stamp and Coin Company. Based on these two sources, it is possible that the 1798 B-31 was discovered in the 1940s.

The Bolender's reference collection (lot 162 in the 1952 sale) stated that the 1800 B-20 (new obverse die, reverse die also used on 1800 B-4 and 1800 B-16) marriage was not known to Haseltine. It also stated that it was "The only piece known to me." Thus it was likely that this die marriage was discovered by Bolender prior to 1950.

The 1802/1 B-9 (new obverse die, reverse previously used on 1801 BB-4 and 1802/1 B-2) was discovered by Bolender in 1950, prior to publication of his book when he purchased the Marmaduke Fox collection. Bolender kept this specimen and it was sold as part of his own reference collection in 1952 where it was purchased by specialist K. P. Austin. Since the discovery, many specimens of B-9 have turned up and been offered for sale.

Summary:

Do you know how many new die marriages of early silver dollars (1794-1803) were discovered in 1997? How many years, prior to 1997, had it been since a new die marriage had been discovered and publicized?

There was one die marriage reported in 1997 but really discovered prior to 1950. It was not included in the 1950 Bolender book. This is the 1795 B-21 (BB-28) discovered by B. G. Johnson as described earlier in this article. There was also the Eliasberg specimen of 1795 B-18 (BB-17) which was "sold" in 1997, and "discovered" in 1953. Thus the correct answer to "How many new die marriages of early silver dollars 1794-1803 were discovered in 1997?" is one. And prior to 1997, the last new die marriage discovered was the 1798 B-33 (BB-117) in 1973, twenty-five years ago!

How many new die marriages have been discovered since M. H. Bolender's *The United States Silver Dollars from 1794 to 1803* was first published in 1950? Since the publication in 1881 of the *Haseltine Type Table?* Who discovered these marriages and when were they first reported?

There are a total of eight new varieties that have been discovered that were not included in the first edition of the Bolender reference. They are 1795 B-21 (BB-28; discovered in the 1930s-40s, surfaced in 1997), 1795 B-18 (BB-17; 1953), 1798 B-32 (BB-91; 1957), 1796 B-6 (BB-64; est. 1956), 1795 B-19 (BB-19; est. 1958-9), 1795 B-20 (BB-16; 1972), 1798 B-33 (BB-117; 1973), and 1795 B-22 (BB-29; 1997). This gives us a grand total of thirteen new varieties of early silver dollars discovered since the *Haseltine Type Table* was first published in 1881!

How many got all the answers right? And did I?

The following article was originally published in the *John Reich Journal* (Volume 11/ Issue 2, January, 1998, pages 6-20) and is reprinted here courtesy of W. David Perkins. Photographs accompanied the original publication. This article won the 1998 Numismatic Literary Guild (NLG) Writer's Competition Best Article Award.

Some Observations About Early Dollars

(Flowing Hair and Draped Bust, 1794-1803)

by John J. Haugh

After two careers and raising four children, I found enough time to return to earlier interests in classic United States coinage. Following brief and intense affairs with Morgan dollars and Indian cents as a collector and part time dealer, I gravitated toward the Flowing Hair and Draped Bust silver dollars of 1794-1803, often collectively referred to herein as Early Dollars (or early dollars). They are now my sole focus.

To more fully appreciate the pivotal role of early dollars in American history (unrealized by virtually everyone, even early dollar "specialists"), one must ponder these points:

The ancient Greek and Roman authorities minted silver coins for nearly 800 years toward the end of the Roman Empire. They were greatly debased, and for most of the Byzantine Empire copper or gold was the medium of exchange. A 900 year tradition of silver coinage began in 755 AD (the year the French government issued silver coins for general use) to the mid 1960s (when governments began to universally replace "hard" money, containing real value, with debased "fiat" coinage) silver took a revered place (alongside gold) as a true "store of value," promoting trade, commerce and a more prosperous populace.

Prior to 1794, trade and commerce in our infant nation were based on barter, foreign coinage of "real" value (e.g. Spanish and Dutch), and/or "paper" currency of dubious value and spotty acceptance (often for good reasons), hindering the growth of a truly "national," interconnected economy.

In 1794, the appearance of "national" silver coinage gave an immensely powerful impetus (both psychological and real) to the prestige and acceptance of the unstable new Federal government, both here and abroad. Enthusiasm for the new national coinage was such that initially, merchants would give more than face "credit" for the new American silver coins. This is not yet fully appreciated by historians (even those with an "economic" viewpoint) or serious students of numismatic history.

The first silver dollars produced in America were the key "linchpin" to each of the above points, though they are often viewed as resting somewhere in a "sleepy backwater" of numismatics (though interest is building at an accelerated pace). As Kenneth Bressett stated in his brilliant foreword to volume one of Q. David Bowers' important encyclopedia on US Silver Dollars, "The dollar [silver coin] is [was] seen as a symbol of the strength and financial power of this nation, and an icon of all that it represents." Small wonder that the beautiful Novodel (a Russian term roughly meaning "new replica") "1804" dollar is widely considered the "King of American coinage," despite its somewhat dubious background!

Regrettably (for numismatics), early dollars have yet to receive the interest and attention they richly deserve. Happily (for those who do understand their true scarcity, diversity and enchantment), they are still obtainable for reasonable sums, compared to their scarcity and true historical position in American coinage—contemplate, for a moment that George Washington undoubtedly had some of the surviving examples in his hands, prior to his demise.

Early Dollars are intriguing. They were our nation's first silver dollars, circulating extensively. Unlike so many of the Morgans—tens of millions of which were simply stored in Mint bags—they do not exist in "pristine" condition. Early dollars are big (39.5mm in diameter) and hefty (26.956 grams). Indeed, they are the largest and heaviest United States silver coins ever minted for general circulation. (This writer sometimes refers to them as The "John Wayne" of American coinage.) Minted on crude machinery and imperfect planchets, with numerous design changes ranging from trivial to major and different die pairings, early dollars offer a seemingly endless challenge. Indeed, despite the passage of over 200 years of existence and several generations of serious analysis, two new distinct die varieties of the 1795 Flowing Hair were identified and widely reported as recently as 1997.

Most early dollars have defects or problems. Some are the result of the crude minting process used at the time (imperfect planchets, adjustment marks, weak strikes, die cracks, rotated sides, clash marks). Some are the result of use or abuse over the past 200 years (e.g. rim dings, scratches, graffiti, retooling, etc.) A good number are holed (many expertly plugged) as early dollars were often used for jewelry, pocket pieces, and (among the elite) as buttons on great-coats. Neither I, nor any specialist I know, has ever seen a perfect one (akin to a Morgan graded MS68), although the Eliasberg 1795 Draped Bust sold in 1987 was awesome. There are so many variables in planchets, striking, rotation, die flaws, and wear that most early dollar specialists concede they have not seen two which were completely identical! Those who migrate from types often found in "pristine" condition are initially shocked. If they stick with it, they learn to accept and appreciate the series, "warts and all."

Proof early dollars do not exist, save for restrikes referred to as "Novodel" dollars, created (clandestinely, in large part) long after production ceased. The "1804" dollar—exquisitely beautiful, though much hyped by dealers and auction firms for five generations—was created decades after the series ended. It is also considered a Novodel dollar, and is referred to by early dollar specialists as a fantasy piece, because it was not part of the regular series (although some wealthy collectors feel they need one to complete their set). The "1804" remains controversial, though specimens continue to set record-breaking prices at auctions; it is considered to be the "most valuable" United States coin. On the other hand, some early dollar collectors contend the term "Novodel" is merely a fancy term for "counterfeit." In this free country, all are allowed to express opinions, but where it matters the most (cash over the table), the "1804" continues to confound its critics, with the beautiful Eliasberg specimen selling for over $1.8 million at a Bowers & Merena auction in 1997. There is an altered "Novedel" 1805 out there somewhere, once owned by famed collector A. J. Ostheimer and later shown by Eric P. Newman who demonstrated it was not "Mint made".

Coin collecting, as we know it today, essentially did not exist in the United States in the late 18th and early 19th centuries. Few early dollars were diverted from circulation. Most experienced extended use (and/or abuse). Well over 90% of the surviving pieces show extensive wear or have some problems, ranging from the trivial to the extreme.

Early Dollar Production and Surival

The Mint's official records indicate a total production of 1,439,196 early dollars bearing the dates 1794 through 1803. Q. David Bowers, in his important treatise on silver dollars, does some rounding, but concludes that 1,431,758 were minted with dates from 1794 through 1803. Both figures include the nearly 20,000 dollars dated 1803, but minted in 1804.

The practice of continuing to produce coins with a previous year's date was common in that era. While there are ongoing debates as to how many early dollars were actually minted with some of the dates, the consensus is that the entire production of all Flowing Hair and Draped Bust (the latter obverse style was adopted in late 1795) was slightly in excess of 1.4 million.

All who have studied early dollars recognize their extremely low survival rate. Walter Breen suggests no more than 4% of the original 1794-1803 mintage survive in all grades. Bowers—who together with Mark Borckardt conducted an extensive study of auctions, collections, and engaged in extensive conferences with specialists—concludes that from 43,000 to 76,000 early dollars remain, suggesting a survival rate of 3 to 5%. These low survival figures include all specimens, regardless of condition (holed, graffiti, scratched, etc.) and wear. No new large hoards have surfaced for decades.

An interesting bit of history which helps one to understand why so many early dollars vanished: On at least two occasions early on in our history (both over 140 years ago), sudden surges in the value of silver created a profit opportunity, prompting many to buy silver dollars (many of which were early dollars) in exchange for paper currency at par. These early dollars were then melted, refined to the necessary (or desirable) purity level, resulting in gain. The tastes and beliefs of the American populace had changed. When early dollars were first introduced, they became the preferred medium of exchange. "Paper" money was then distrusted—most history buffs recall the popular comment, early in American history, when defaults on government obligations were fresh in the memories of the populace—to refer to an item of little or no value as, "not worth a Continental."

In their own peculiar way, the success of the first silver dollars series sowed the seed of its own demise by increasing confidence in government "money." As the Federal government developed a better reputation for stability—and commercial activity increased commensurate with American expansion—heavy coinage became less desirable than lightweight "paper" money in higher denominations. "Checks" drawn on banks could be generally relied on. The revered silver dollar, heavy and difficult to move around in quantity, became less favored.

The populace became not only willing, but actually anxious, to exchange their heavy, clumsy silver dollars for paper money, at par. The French in particular were adept at seizing the opportunity, engaging agents in the United

States to buy up early dollars and other US silver coinage. They were then melted, refined, and reminted into silver French coins. While that is not the only reason why so few early dollars now survive, it was a major contributing factor. Indeed, a detailed study of all the socioeconomic factors which contributed to the present dearth of classic US silver coinage, especially in higher grades, is worthy of an entire book.

For present, many factors combined for roughly 96% of all early dollars ever minted to disappear. The absence of sufficient numbers (by date, variety, or major variety) of these coins has, in turn, led to disinterest in them on "electronic" trading networks (not enough are available in comparable grades to make an active market) and to the popular "bid" prices quoted in the graysheet being almost pathetically below the real market for sound. There is virtually no advertising and/or major promotions of early dollars by major dealers because they simply cannot obtain sufficient numbers of early dollars to justify the expense and effort involved, which they commonly do with Morgan/Peace dollars and other more plentiful "types." Hence, a smaller number of collectors take the time to become enchanted enough with the series to seriously commit to it—though that number is growing significantly.

To put the relative scarcity of all early dollars in perspective, compare the entire series mintage (1794 through 1803) of 1.4 million with one date/mint of the Morgan series, the 1881-S, which was 12.7 million (and far from the highest). The relative scarcity of "Mint State" early dollars is even more dramatic. Two of the certification services (PCGS and NGC) have graded over 170,000 1881-S Morgans to be "Mint State" (MS60 or higher), whereas less than 300 early dollars from the entire series have been graded Mint State by those same two services. Even that figure—roughly 287 as of mid 1998—is inflated because of resubmissions. Stated differently, a Mint State 1881-S is over 500 times more common than any Mint State early dollar from the entire series.

Buttressing those who believe in a survival rate for the whole ten year series at the low end of estimates (35,000 to 50,000 total survivors) is the low survival of the 1794. Of the documented mintage of 1,758 pieces, most estimates are that 125-135 have survived. No mintage year of the entire early dollar series has been as extensively studied as the 1794. Among others, the late Jack Collins exhaustively studied the 1794 for some two decades. He was assisted by leading specialists, including Martin Oghigian and Jules Reiver. At the time of Collins' untimely demise, 125 known specimens had been identified, (although a few of those might be duplicates, as so many 1794 pieces were doctored over the decades. The Collins manuscript for a book on the 1794 mintage, nearly completed when he died, has never been published. It is the near unanimous belief of early dollar specialists that there could not be more than 150 survivors of the 1794 issue.

The 1794 was mostly distributed to high government officials and members of Congress, and was the first dollar coin ever struck in the US. Less than only 8.5% of the 1794 mintage survive. It is reasonable to assume the survival rate of the 1794 is at least twice the balance of the entire series. It is logical, therefore, to accept Breen's opinion that no more than 4% of the entire early dollar production of 1.4 million have survived (less than 56,000). This writer concurs with the consensus of early dollar specialists that no more than 45,000 ± survive today (in any condition).

Uncertified (Raw) vs. Certified Early Dollars

The argument between proponents of uncertified and certified (coins encased in plastic holders, graded by independent services which issue limited guarantees) will probably never end. Though the early copper collectors are the most vocal of collector groups opposed to these holders, early dollar enthusiasts are a close second. Many early dollar collectors and specialists remain adamantly opposed to "certification."

Certified proponents argue holders have reduced counterfeits, made grading more consistent, and have curbed the tendency to "buy the coin as VF, sell as XF-AU," as well as given collectors and investors more confidence. Opponents of certification argue the process siphons needed money from the hobby, leads to holder worship, encourages hair splitting between grades, and encourages coin doctors to make minor adjustments, then cover up their handiwork through adding artificially dark toning (or other masks), and have coins upgraded by services. Moreover, many early dollar collectors—especially those used to being able to handle and feel their coins, as well as examine the rims and lettered edges—believe strongly that holders inhibit the joy of owning and examining them.

Holders do preclude the examination of the edge lettering and the outer edge of the rims. A number of collectors will buy early dollars in holders, then "crack" them out. Each side's vocal advocates can recount anecdotal, true horror stories to back up their positions. Opponents of certification can, for example, point to certified coins sold by reputable auction houses as "AU" which are now in "MS" holders. Proponents can recount true incidents of uncertified early dollars catalogued as AU, or sold at that grade by dealers, which later proved to be holed and plugged, clearly a lesser grade, or even counterfeit.

This writer belongs to neither camp; buying, selling and stocking both uncertified and certified. The most sensible alternative is to follow the maxim "buy the coin, not the holder." The trend of the market clearly favors certification for more expensive and scarcer coins. But, as one wry observer quipped recently, "They [the certification services] won't really prevail, if ever [with regard to early dollars] until there's an awful lot of funerals."

I found it both perplexing and amusing to recently watch a self-proclaimed sophisticated collector carefully examine certified Draped Bust Dollars from only two services (PCGS and NGC). After much time spent studying several coins under magnification, he paid a premium for a lovely 1800 in a NGC holder. Then he loudly announced he despised holders, explaining he would crack the coin out of the NGC holder. Yet he had completely ignored uncertified specimens, and ANACS certified coins of the same variety—clearly of better quality—at less cost in the same case. That collector, a nationally prominent expert in his own field of endeavor who has collected and studied early dollars for over two decades, was relying on the judgment of others (graders) who may have half his knowledge and experience.

Have We Seen Inflation or Deflation of Early Dollar Grading Over the Past Fifteen Years?

Some specialists who have carefully followed the Flowing Hair/Bust dollar series over the past three to five decades, can easily document that grading standards have "relaxed" or "loosened" over that time period. They point to examples of early dollars, appearing raw in sales—especially from 1930 to 1980, graded XF to AU then—which are now in certified holders, ten to fifteen points higher. Opinions vary as to why this has occurred. The converse is also true. Those who contend that grading standards have in fact "tightened" can point to examples previously graded uncertified as "AU" which are now in VF/XF holders.

Certification services were more conservative ten-fifteen years ago than now, though there are notable exceptions. Some ascribe the trend to a conspiracy, where certification services routinely loosen and tighten standards, simply to induce more resubmissions, thus increasing their fee income. Some point out wide discrepancies between the same varieties, clearly of the same quality, from the same service, suggesting greed, avarice and/or favoritism. Others point out that grading is part science and part art, with much of it being subjective. Some dramatic discrepancies are the result of grader inexperience and/or grader "turnover" at the services.

Compounding the controversy, some coin doctors can enhance the look of high grade coins, including early dollars, which have lots of detail (they say "meat"). A coin this writer sold in one holder as AU50 (a fair grade) was shown to me four months later, in an AU58 holder (different service), toned much darker. Laser technology, powerful scopes, miniature tools and "luster enhancing" chemicals are sometimes used to try to upgrade a coin. But, such efforts also often fail, or result in a lower grade. Nevertheless, view certified early dollars—especially those graded AU53 to MS63 and darkly toned—skeptically and carefully. On the other hand, many darkly toned, high grade specimens became that way naturally because of age and/or environmental factors.

Other notables, including Bowers, contend that grading has tightened since certification took hold, leading to more careful scrutiny, better standards, and more uniformity. They can point to numerous examples to prove their point. This writer remains neutral on the point, though in agreement with most of the arguments made by stalwarts on each side of the issue.

Though many conspiracy theories abound, I have yet to meet a professional grader or cataloguer who did not convey a genuine dedication to doing the best, most accurate job possible. My personal belief—certainly not shared by all—is that much of the alleged "grade inflation" in the early dollar arena is primarily due to more experience and knowledge about weak strikes, imperfect planchets, and other flaws found in the Flowing Hair/Bust dollar series, as well as to graders seeing more examples because of increased volume/turnover (compounded by air travel and overnight services).

Holder Envy

In early 1998, the pecking order among the competitive services, in terms of collector/dealer interest, is PCGS, NGC, ANACS, and PCI. In a perfect, sensible world all experienced collectors should buy the coin for its strike, eye appeal, and overall condition, regardless of status (certified or uncertified) or holder brand. The true early dollar specialists who have labored in the vineyards for years (or decades) largely follow the sensible precept "Buy the coin, not the status (certified or uncertified) or holder brand." Regardless of which service one prefers (or abhors), all should give careful consideration to that precept, more often spoken than followed. Novices understandably prefer certified early dollars, because they do come with a limited guarantee.

Much of the special cachet given to PCGS and NGC holders is due to innovative marketing and advertising. Although ANACS is generally placed third in the dealer/collector interest pecking order, some who see the most early dollars concede (privately) that it is the most consistent grading service with regard to early dollars. Some of the best buys this writer is aware of come when specialists cherry pick early dollars in PCI holders, though some react to that brand holder as though it contains a dangerous contagion. The best possible advice remains the same as always, buy the coin, not the holder!

Cleaned and Dipped Early Dollars

In the early years of coin collecting/accumulating, it was a common practice—indeed, encouraged—to lightly clean and/or lightly dip coins. This was routinely done to remove dirt, grime, debris, and ugly toning—as well as add luster and/or improve eye appeal. As the United States' oldest dollar coinage, most early dollars have been subjected to at least light cleaning and/or light dipping one or more times in their 200 year (plus or minus) history. On various occasions, light burnishing or whizzing was even considered acceptable or tolerable. As tastes changed, and a more sophisticated understanding and appreciation of coins in their natural state became the norm, those practices have become inappropriate to unacceptable.

Contrary to popular belief, all services will holder and grade (without net grading down) Flowing Hair and Bust Dollars that have been lightly cleaned and/or lightly dipped. They generally draw the line at coins where the cleaning/dipping has been conducted in such a way that the fields have been damaged (hairlines visible under low magnification, fields dull, and/or lifeless because of harsh treatment). Some insist the distinction is without a difference. Others argue a line has to be drawn somewhere. This writer surveyed fourteen collectors and dealers who see and handle a large number of Flowing Hair and Draped Bust dollars, asking two simple questions, for both certified and raw example:

Question

How many early dollars have been lightly cleaned at onetime in their past?

Answers Averaged

Raw	Certified
79%	76%

Question

2. How many early dollars have been dipped at one time in their past?

Answers Averaged

Raw	Certified
74%	71%

Those who are most knowledgeable feel nearly all early dollars have been lightly cleaned and/or lightly dipped at one point, whether uncertified or certified. With combined (cumulative) early dollar experience of over 350 years, one can assume the consensus of those fourteen is close to reality.

A good number of surviving early dollars have, at some point, been harshly cleaned (leaving hairlines and/or disturbing the "fields"). Most services will not "holder" these, others will "net grade" down to what they perceive the market level to be at that time (e.g. "XF details, cleaned and tooled, net VF25), or note the specific "defects." Nevertheless, as one witty early dollar specialist observed, "I scoop those up too, especially the R-5 to R-8 specimens. After all, it [harsh cleaning] ain't the coin's fault." Varieties with hairlines or other obvious signs of harsh cleaning, rated R-5 or higher are often moved briskly, usually at a premium. Common varieties (R-1 to R-3) with similar defects trade at a discount. Nicer early dollars in general trade well above graysheet bid prices.

The editors of the "Coin Dealer" newsletter (popularly referred to as the graysheet), whose figures are obviously below the real market for better specimens, defend their figures as a fair average. They point out that early dollars are scarce, infrequently appearing on electronic bid/want/ask services or in auctions. There are so many variables, varieties, and different rarity ratings within specific years that averaging prices for early dollars would be a daunting task. It is nigh impossible to buy better quality early dollars at or below sheet, as they trade above graysheet averages—often at large premiums—depending on condition, eye appeal, and rarity.

The few coin doctors who employ advanced technology to make minor changes to early dollar coins and/or add luster to surfaces, often attempt to cover evidence of their handiwork. Most graders, acutely aware of that practice, now more closely examine coins with a high grade look but unusual or overly dark toning, rejecting many. A few nevertheless slip through, and a good number of upgraded early dollars (especially those graded from 1993-97) remain available in the market. Before purchasing darkly-toned early dollars or those with unusual coloring in high grade holders (AU55 to MS63), examine them carefully under a binocular (some use a spectrum) scope, or have a specialist do so for you.

Damages, Retooled and Repaired Early Dollars

A good number—experts opine 20% to 35% of the Flowing Hair and Bust Dollars which survive—have been damaged or abused, then reworked (holed and later plugged, initials or scratches removed, weakly struck and/or worn areas enhanced, as well as messed with to improve denticles and mask or eliminate rim dings). Most such prior handiwork is obvious under magnification or binocular (some use a spectrum) scope examination. Major auction firms carefully describe such tampering to avoid coins being returned, and to protect their reputations. The same is true for most dealers specializing in early dollars. Despite care, some slip through such scrutiny and end up in holders.

In general, early dollars with such damage and repairs trade at a discount, especially the more common varieties (R-1 through R-3). Those quite scarce or truly rare (R-5 through R-8) often trade more briskly, even though damaged, abused, and/or expertly (or crudely) repaired. The elusive 1794 trades quickly, regardless of defects. Some holed early dollars have been so expertly plugged that the repair is virtually impossible to detect, especially when retoned (naturally or artificially). Early dollars with graffiti (initials, scratched Xs, names of ships, etc.) are heavily discounted, but some collectors actively seek those with lovely counterstamps, initials, and/or major defects.

Counterfeits

Counterfeit early dollars are encountered, especially the 1794 Flowing Hair, the 1799 Draped Bust, and the 1804 Novodel Draped Bust (many 1801s have been reingraved to make the "1" a "4"). Some counterfeits are quite remarkable, blessed as genuine by advanced experts (see Reiver's discussion of two identical 1794s, each with ANA authenticity certifications, one of which is obviously a near perfect replica of the other, in text of this work). Some counterfeits have the exact weight, fineness, and size of genuine counterparts, achieved by melting an inexpensive common variety, and producing a perfectly genuine planchet. That planchet is then used to replicate a rare date or variety. Fortunately, such unusually expert counterfeits are themselves quite scarce. Any reputable dealer or auction house will promptly reimburse purchasers of early dollars—later shown to be counterfeit—in full.

Seasoned early dollar veterans uniformly advise all to examine the purchases and know who they are dealing with. On the other hand, when offered true rarities in early dollar series at price levels absurdly below market, one should skeptically and critically examine the proposed purchase, obtaining independent opinions.

Do not allow the few downsides of the fascinating and exciting Flowing Hair and Draped Bust Dollar series (which is the case for all type) interfere with the joy and challenges it presents. early dollars occupy a special place in the history of our country as well as the evolvement of our coinage system. They are perhaps the most fascinating type one could focus on, and will give the casual collector, the advanced collector, as well as the specialists much joy and fascination.

Special Note Regarding Rarity Ratings

Rarity ratings are the considered judgment of the person compiling them, based on personal observations and the considered opinions of colleagues. They are both subjective and objective. As more collections and individual specimens have come onto the market and have been sold through the auctions (being carefully described and/or photographed), rarity ratings have changed over the years. They are fluid, always subject to revision. The rarity ratings used throughout this discussion were developed by W. David Perkins of Colorado, a noted early dollar specialist. They reflect his latest opinion, as of the Spring of 1998. I find them reliable and consistent with my own experience.

Sources

BOOKS AND LITERATURE:

Bolender, M. H., *The United States Early Silver Dollars, From 1794 to 1803* (Reiver Revision, 4th Edition, Krause, 1958).

Bowers, Q. David, *Silver Dollars & Trade Dollars of the United States,* Vol. One (Bowers and Merena Galleries, Inc., 1993).

Breen, Walter, *Complete Encyclopedia of U.S. and Colonial Coins* (Doubleday, 1988).

Bressett, Kenneth E., "The Baffling Case of the Plugged Dollars," *The Numismatist*, March, 1993.

Bressett, Kenneth E., "1795 United States Silver Dollar with Official Plug," paper delivered to American Numismatic Society (Oct. 30, 1993); "Coin World" (numerous issues, 1969-1997).

Haseltine, John W.," Type Table Catalogue" (in Haseltine Sale Catalogue, 1881). "Numismatic News" (numerous issues 1973-1998), published by Krause Publications, Iola, Wisconsin.

Pilliod, Chris, "1795 Half Dollar with Center Plug" (Privately published, August 1997). "Rare Coin Review" (numerous issues, 1984-1998), Bowers and Merena, Wolfeboro, N.H.

Raymond, Wayte, "Descriptive List of Die Varieties of Early Silver Dollars," Coin and Medal Bulletin, 1916.

Yeoman, R. S., *Guide Book to United States Coins, 1997 Edition* (Whitman, 1988).

INTERVIEWS: Extensive interviews were conducted with dozens of coin dealers, Early Dollar specialists, and numismatic historians (some of whom wish to remain anonymous). Among the individuals interviewed were: Jules Reiver, W. David Perkins, Jim Matthews, Russell Logan, Lano Balulescu, Chris Pilliod, Martin Oghigian, Tate Chesbrough, Bob Merrill, Jim McGuigan, Martin Mansfield, Steve Fischer, Mark Borckardt, Jack Beymer, Rob Retz, Coleman Foster, George Eggimann, and David and John Feigenbaum. Although indebted to all of the above (and others), the author is especially grateful to Messrs Reiver, Perkins, Matthews, Oghigian, Borckardt, and McGuigan for their sharing of insight and experience. The opinions expressed above are mine, not theirs. Undoubtedly, each would dissent from one or more. As a noted numismatic historian once exclaimed, "Differing opinions help keep the hobby interesting."

Countermarked and Overstruck Early U.S. Dollars

by: Robert Stark

"Those of us who have wandered down the numismatic byroad that leads to the study of countermarks occasionally find ourselves far from the beaten path. Bogged down in a quagmire of uncertainty. Fanciful conjecture sometimes influences our attempts to decipher some obscure hieroglyphic impressed upon a coin by an individual in some perilous time past."

So wrote Edward Fisher in last month's *Numismatist,* in an article dealing with 19th century Mexican countermarks—and it somewhat applies here. About two years ago, I saw a few countermarks on early dollars and made a note of them. My interest had less to do with countermarks than with the usage to which our early dollars were put since I have collected them for many years. Several dozen countermarks have come to my attention since—and for some there is a history of sorts—but for the most part they pose questions to which I lack answers.

As information accumulates you classify. These four classifications have been useful:

Personal pocket pieces.
Value certification.
Merchant advertising.
Endorsing local use.

Many of the countermarked early dollars bear initials. As you can imagine, this is a difficult group. Personal pocket pieces would seem to be in this group.

A 1799 dollar with the initials FW and 1863 in script and a less fancy B and C is an example. Could it have been carried by a Union soldier? And if it was...you can imagine the questions we might have; especially since by 1863, a 1799 dollar was a "keeper".

Do Countermarked Names Give Us Better Prospects?

W.B. Joy on a 1798 dollar—but who was W. B. Joy?

M. Miner also on a 1798 dollar—but as yet no clue!

A. Goddard on an 1800 dollar.

If these people were merchants or otherwise prominent, it is likely that they will eventually be identified because of the microfilm availability of earlier newspapers, city directories, and the like.

L. L. Squire on a 1795 dollar is probably the work of L.L. Squire and Sons, ship chandlers and rope makers on Front Street in New York. Besides rope and candles, the firm dealt in oils, paints, anchors, chain cables. And naval stores.

C. C. Clark, Carlos C. Clark, appears on a 1799 and on an 1802 dollar. Clark, a New England gunsmith seems to have had a penchant for recording dates on early dollars. The dates could relate to his career. On the 1802 dollar there are three dates, 1842, 1864, and 1879 and an engraved flower. Russell Rulau conjectures that he began self-employment in Windsor, VT as a gunsmith in 1842. There are records that he was employed from 1846 to 1856 by percussion rifle makers Robbins and Lawrence. He moved to New Hampshire about 1863, and possibly the 1864b date in the coin refers to the actual date of relocation. The 1879 date may indicate retirement. A 1799 dollar, apparently using the same or similar punches, bears his name and the dates 1842 to 1879.

Whether these are personal pocket pieces or advertisements I don't know.

Abram Brinsmaid, a Burlington, VT silversmith, was born in Great Barrington, MA in 1770 and died in Burlington in 1811. His firm and its successors, Brinsmaid and Hildreth, used this hall mark years after his death. The same hallmark is known on silverware, in addition to this double struck 1795 flowing hair dollar. This dollar is the most prominent double strike I've ever seen on an early dollar, and it is a very rare die variety (Bolender-8) of which only a few are known. It has occurred to me that since the mint often delivered coins in exchange for a like weight of bullion, that possibly the production of this rare variety went to the Burlington area.

This H. G. Stone hallmark on an 1803 dollar is attributed to Hubbard Stone, a New York silversmith.

"**EB counterstamp,** fodder for legends," is the lead line on a *Coin World* article in 1992 by Bill Swoger. These are the doubloon and the George III Guinea. These represent Ephriam Brasher's trade of certifying foreign gold coins for use here. The New York goldsmith lived from 1744-1810 (and counted George Washington among his circle). Note that as initialed coins, these fit a personal piece category. As a known hallmark, they fit the advertising category. And as assays of sorts they fit the certification for value and even the authorization for local use categories. So much for any thoughts of an unambiguous classification.

The fame of the EB countermark tempts some to attribute all of them to Brasher. Milfred Bolender's early dollar book has been a valuable standard for many years—although it is now inadequate. Bolender attributes this 1799 dollar with an EB countermark to Brasher. But some point out that Brasher may have only countermarked gold coins. Gregory Brunk, regarded as the foremost student of countermarks, asserts that not all the EB countermarks seen on many coins belong to Brasher. He suggests that this one in particular may belong to Ezekiel Burr, a Providence silversmith who dies in 1846.

But, is it Ezekiel Burr? An authoritative volume by Belden on Early American Silver lists and attributes EB hall marks to various silversmiths. A bit of detective work probably can settle this. As more suggestions were made of what different EB's stand for, I began to think it stood for Every Body.

L. Bailey on a 1795 bust dollar is attributed, by Brunk to a Lebbus Bailey, a Portland, ME, gunsmith. Dave Bowers thinks this could be the mark of Loring Bailey, a Hingham (or Hull), MA, silversmith of the period. Dave's thought is prompted by the hallmark; it was more likely to be used by a silversmith than a gunsmith. I think the piece supports a conjecture that a coin could be a handy piece on which to try a new punch or puncher. It follows that writing off all EB's not on gold as not belonging to Brasher may be hasty.

Finally, among the merchants, is everybody's favorite, Houck's Panacea. This half dollar belongs to the Smithsonian, as well as this 1795 flowing hair dollar. This is an ad from an early Baltimore City Directory, and some 150 years later, medicine is still trying to achieve Houck's Panacea.

The countermarking by silversmiths seems to be a practice of those in the northeast. I can't recall any south of New York, and most are from New England.

British merchants certified value in local currency. The splendid mark of Scottish Copper and Coal Co. of John Wilson appears on this 1800 dollar that belongs to the ANS, the gift of Mrs. Norweb in 1967. Note the 5 shilling value and the Scottish town of Hurlet.

Two other merchant countermarks are known. One belonging to John McLean on a 1799 dollar with inscribed value 5 shillings, 3 pence and the Scottish town of Paisley.

The third such is countermarked " WG and CO" and four shillings, nine pence, and is also attributed to a Scottish merchant.

That all three known merchant pieces are from Scotland, in view of the severe British coin shortage about that time, suggests that the officially counterstamped George III pieces didn't reach the Scot's in adequate quantities.

Turning to countermarks and overstrikes that may be attributed to official bodies, or perhaps, counterfeiters.

In the last years of the eighteenth century and in the early 1800s, Britain experienced a severe shortage of circulating silver, as I noted. The British possessed sizable quantities of captured Spanish dollars and as an attempt to relieve the shortage, the king's head, used to mark silver, was stamped on the head of the Spanish king, Charles IV in March 1797. These were to be valued at 4 shillings and 6 pence each.

However, before issue it was discovered that the bullion value was 4 and 8; a melt value of two pence higher that the intended facade value. Simple solution: to prevent melting, revalue them at 4 and 9. About 2-1/2 million, were issued according to Howland Wood, an early student of the subject. The issue was immediately counterfeited which seems to give credence to a couplet of the time, "The Bank to make the Spanish dollar, stamped the head of a fool on the head of an ass." The issue was demonetized, in May 1804.

A new dollar was announced that a Mr. Boulton of Soho Mint fame had been engaged to produce by obliterating the Spanish markings. This 5 shilling dollar, Bank of England, 1804 about Britannia and with a George III obverse and this Bank of Ireland 6 shilling dollar belong to the ANS.

The relevance of all this, is that while the official act applied only to the Spanish dollars, an oval George III countermark appears on a 1795 flowing hair dollar and octagonal impressions (intended to make counterfeiting more difficult) are known on 1798 and 1799 dollars. What isn't known is whether or not these royal countermarks on U. S. dollars are counterfeits possibly intended to aid foreign coinage to pass more readily. An early Bangs Auction shows the royal countermark on a U.S. 1795 half-dollar. Contemporary counterfeits are uninteresting; but counterfeits of the time were, after all, circulating coinage.

Much U.S. coinage circulated or was melted south of our border. Indeed, some believe that President Jefferson halted dollar production at least in part because of such melting.

An "R. F. 1845" countermark has appeared on several dates, including an 1800 dollar. It has been suggested that these could have been made for the French Caribbean, say Guadeloupe; the R. F. standing for "Republique Francais". Brunk is adamant that these are fantasy pieces that never saw the Caribbean. It's possible that some of the support for Caribbean usage came from a French edict of 1802 for Guadeloupe that silver dollar-sized coins have octagonal sections cut from the center and stamped "4E" (for the local currency) and "R. F."

The "fleur des lis" on this holed 1800 dollar owned by the ANS. The box in which it is housed has a notation to the effect that it was counterstamped by decree of the Governor General on November 27, 1884, and "the collectors of customs at Fajardo, Guayama, Ponce, Mayaguez, Arecibo, Vieques, and San Juan counterstamped them to validate the holed coins then in circulation." It seems a very large date for a circulating early dollar!

Further south to Uruguay, during a nine year siege of Montevideo (1843-1852) pesos were struck on our early dollars. Two examples are known. One is on a 1799 dollar recently sold by Superior Galleries and the other on a 1798 dollar that is owned by the ANS.

Now I will conclude with two 1794 dollars. First, this note in the *Numismatist* in 1947 was brought to my attention by John Kleeberg. A 1794 dollar countermarked "F 7°" to stand for Ferdinand the 7th apparently for use in the Phillipines, then, of course, under Spanish rule. A note in a 1949 *Numismatist* indicates that the coin was among other loot offered for sale in California. Its current whereabouts are unknown to me.

Second, a 1795 dollar (Bolender) 4, struck over a 1794 dollar that belongs to Bowers and Merena. The obverse clearly shows the outline of the eagle, wreath, and parts of the United.

The reverse shows some profile and the back of Liberty's head. The coin was discovered by Breen. Walter speculates on its origins in a 1961 issue of the *Metropolitan Numismatic Journal.* I have some recollection that he once entertained the idea that the mint may have struck a round number of 1794 dollars, say 2000 pieces. The reported mintage of 1758 pieces, nearly none of high quality, may be all that were judges even marginally useful as coinage. This piece, struck so weakly, kept it from the melting pot to await proper coin press next year.

So many people have helped me that it is hard to know where to start or end. I relied on Jules Reiver for many slides and checking information and theories with him became almost a daily ritual. I'd occasionally get a call about countermarks from someone and I'd be amused to hear that John Kleeberg referred them. I don't know why, because most of what I know, I learned from him. He's been a fountain of information for me. Greg Brunk, in books and in person, has been very helpful and generous. As for the several others, I'll have to thank them in print.

1795 - B8 - BRINSMAIDS - (BELDEN PAGE 76)

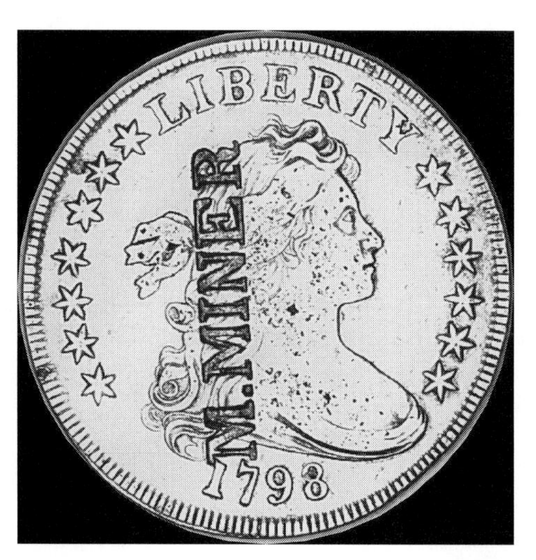

1798 - B4 - M. MINER

1798 - B23 - W.B. JOY

1800 - B11 - A. GODDARD

1803 - B4 - H. G. STONE (BELDEN P396)

1799 - B10 - 1863 - JW - BC

About the Author

A resident of Wilmington, Delaware, Jules Reiver was born in 1916 and has been actively collecting coins since 1923. Jules became a collector at the age of seven, when his father gave him an accumulation of assorted coins which he had over the years dropped into a wooden cigar box—because they were old or unusual , like 20-cent pieces—kept alongside the cash register in his home furnishings store.

Jules began assimilating the accumulation into collections by series at an early age, graduating from one series to another as the earlier pursuits were completed. He collected everything in minors and silver coins except dollars, which he felt were too expensive to pursue. As the years passed, Reiver met a Wilmington stock broker, Laird Townsend, who collected early dollars and encouraged him to expand his horizons into that realm as well.

Attending a September 18, 1968, Lester Merkin sale, in pursuit of an 1805 dated addition to his variety collection of early US half dimes, Reiver failed to realize his objective, when the auctioneer, after first knocking the coin down to him, reopened bidding and awarded the coin to a telephone bidder. Having lost out on the half dime, Jules decided that rather than be shut out on the sale, he would bid on some early dollars that came up later in the sale.

The Merkin sale offerings featured half of the Ostheimer collection of Bust Dollars, including some quite rare ones. Ostheimer had consigned the coins to Merkin for sale subsequent to the other half having been stolen. Reiver was an active and successful bidder for the nucleus of the early dollar offerings on this occasion.

Actually, an unusual twist of fate was responsible for this beginning of Jules' pursuit of early dollars. Subsequent to having commissioned Merkin to sell half of his Bust Dollar collection, Ostheimer had regained possession of the stolen half, when the thief could not sell the coins and ransomed them back to their rightful owner. Having published the catalog of the sale, Merkin declined a solicitation from Ostheimer to remove his Bust Dollar consignment from the sale. Ostheimer's only avenue for reassembling the collection at that point was to bid them in at the sale, which he declined to do.

The stolen and recovered half of the Ostheimer collection of Bust Dollars was sold by Superior at its August 20, 1975, ANA sale, with Reiver being the purchaser of quite a few of them. Jules had filled some additional critical blanks in his forming collection with purchases made at the Spies sale conducted in December, 1974, by Stack's.

Reiver's early dollars collection presently numbers 113 of the 116 documented varieties, lacking only the 1795 B18, B20, and B21 varieties. Also missing, of course, are the several questionable coins which have been reported through the years, but not confirmed.

Appendix A:

Location Numbers for Heraldic Eagle Dollars Reverse Dies

A few years ago, my friend Eric Newman asked for a method to determine if other reverse dies than those we knew of, were used on both gold and other coins in the early years. I suggested a numbering system which could be used on all of the Heraldic Eagle reverses.

Here are the numbers for all of the early dollars with the Heraldic Eagle reverses. The four points covered are the ones usually used to check the reverses:

#1 is the relation of the 12th star and the Eagle's beak.

#2 is the location of the tip of the leaf under the I in AMERICA to the bottom of the I.

3 is the relation of the leaf under C in AMERICA to the C.

#4 is the relation of the berry under the second A in AMERICA to the A.

In using the system, don't try to make each number exact. Put each digit down as most probable, then others which are close. It should narrow down the field. Let me know of any glaring errors.

1798

1 2 2 3	B9
1 2 3 4	B11, B15, B16, B27
1 3 2 4	B3, B7, B20
1 3 3 5	B18, B22
1 4 3 4	B13, B21
1 4 4 5	B19, B23
1 5 4 6	B10
1 5 5 6	B28
2 5 4 6	B5
3 3 3 5	B30
3 4 3 5	B14
3 5 4 5	B24, B25
3 5 4 6	B26
3 5 4 6	B31
3 5 4 6	B33
4 4 3 5	B4, B32
4 5 4 5	B6, B17
5 5 4 6	B8
5 5 5 6	B12, B29

1799

3 5 4 5	B15
3 5 4 6	B7
3 5 4 6	B13
4 5 3 5	B3, B4
5 4 3(5)	B16, B23, B12, B11
(the berries disappear on this die)	
5 4 3 5	B10
5 4 3 5	B17
5 5 3 5	B18
5 5 4 5	B5
5 5 4 6	B1
5 5 4 6	B8
5 5 4 6	B14, B21
5 5 4 6	B22
5 5 5 7	B6
5 5 5 7	B9
6 5 3 5	B2, B19

1800

3 5 4 6	B17
4 4 3 5	B12
4 5 4 5	B5, B10
4 5 5 6	B8
4 5 5 6	B15
4 5 5 7	B4, B16, B20
5 5 4 6	B11, B19
5 5 4 6	B13
5 5 4 6	B14
5 5 5 6	B3
5 6 5 7	B1, B2

1801

3 4 3 4	B2
3 5 5 6	B4
3 5 5 6	B3
5 5 4 5	B1
5 5 5 6	B5

1802

3 4 3 4	B1, B4, B6
3 5 5 6	B2, B3, B5, B9
5 5 5 6	B8

1803

3 4 3 4	B4, B6

HERALDIC EAGLE SILVER DIES

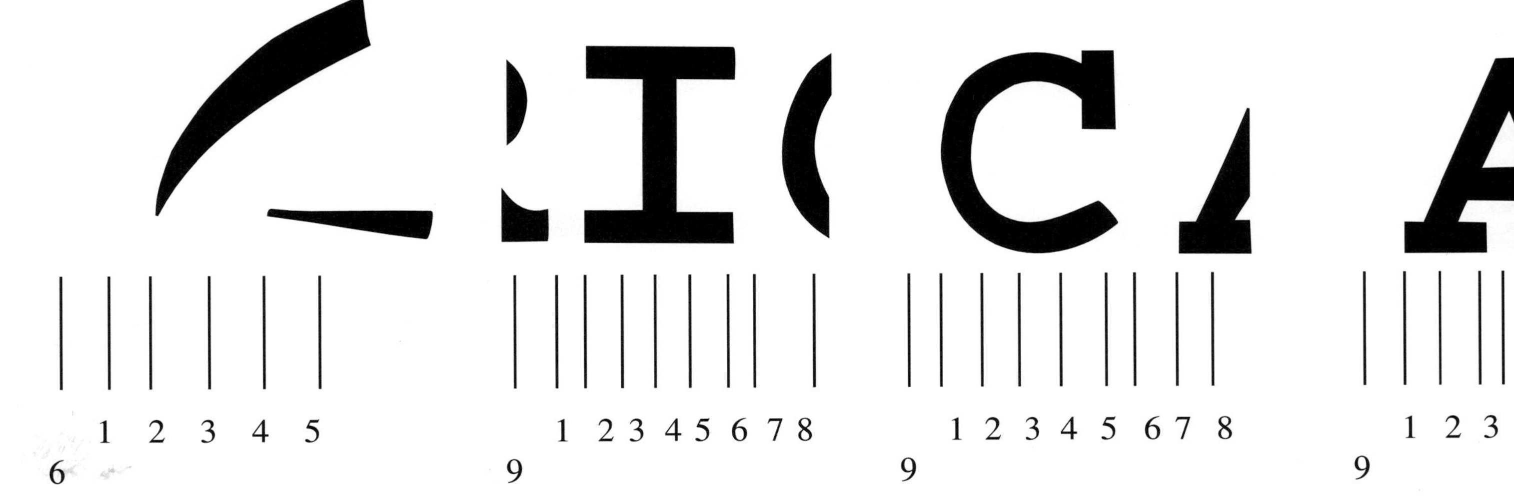

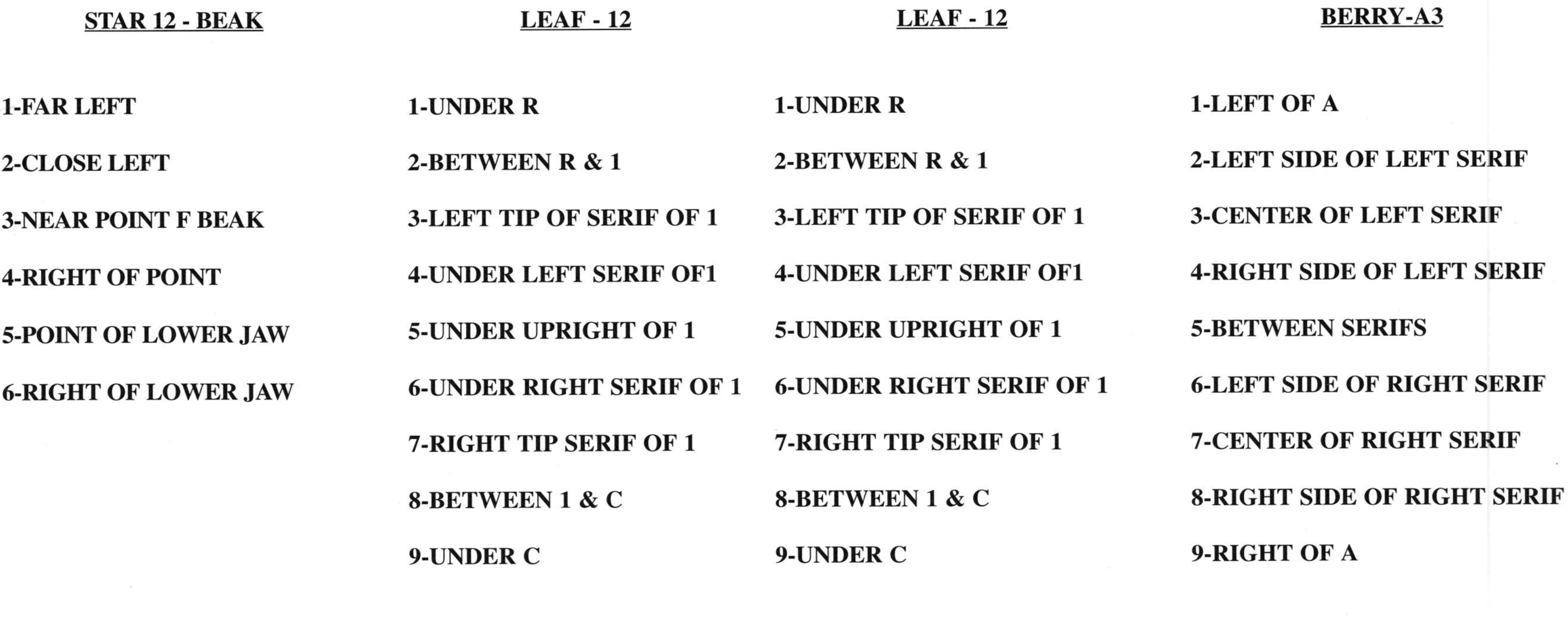

STAR 12 - BEAK

1-FAR LEFT
2-CLOSE LEFT
3-NEAR POINT F BEAK
4-RIGHT OF POINT
5-POINT OF LOWER JAW
6-RIGHT OF LOWER JAW

LEAF - 12

1-UNDER R
2-BETWEEN R & 1
3-LEFT TIP OF SERIF OF 1
4-UNDER LEFT SERIF OF1
5-UNDER UPRIGHT OF 1
6-UNDER RIGHT SERIF OF 1
7-RIGHT TIP SERIF OF 1
8-BETWEEN 1 & C
9-UNDER C

LEAF - 12

1-UNDER R
2-BETWEEN R & 1
3-LEFT TIP OF SERIF OF 1
4-UNDER LEFT SERIF OF1
5-UNDER UPRIGHT OF 1
6-UNDER RIGHT SERIF OF 1
7-RIGHT TIP SERIF OF 1
8-BETWEEN 1 & C
9-UNDER C

BERRY-A3

1-LEFT OF A
2-LEFT SIDE OF LEFT SERIF
3-CENTER OF LEFT SERIF
4-RIGHT SIDE OF LEFT SERIF
5-BETWEEN SERIFS
6-LEFT SIDE OF RIGHT SERIF
7-CENTER OF RIGHT SERIF
8-RIGHT SIDE OF RIGHT SERIF
9-RIGHT OF A